Joshua Fraser

Shanty, Forest and River Life in the Backwoods of Canada

Joshua Fraser

Shanty, Forest and River Life in the Backwoods of Canada

ISBN/EAN: 9783744791199

Printed in Europe, USA, Canada, Australia, Japan

Cover: Foto ©Andreas Hilbeck / pixelio.de

More available books at **www.hansebooks.com**

Cutting the High Fall's Dam.

SHANTY, FOREST AND RIVER LIFE

IN THE

BACKWOODS OF CANADA.

BY THE

Author of "Three Months Among the Moose."

MONTREAL:
PRINTED BY JOHN LOVELL & SON.
1883.

DEDICATED,

BY PERMISSION,

TO THE RIGHT HONORABLE

SIR JOHN A. MACDONALD, K.C.B.,

With profound respect,

BY

THE AUTHOR.

CONTENTS.

CHAPTERS.
I.	Reminiscences, Reflections	7
II.	Manahan's Shanty and Surroundings	16
III.	Shanty Government	26
IV.	"I'll roast the Devil out of you"	35
V.	A Merry Old Cook	43
VI.	"My Home! my Home! my Home!"	57
VII.	Old Saint-Saint, the Hermit	64
VIII.	Forest Fires	75
IX.	A Sunday Service in the Shanty	96
X.	Gentlemen Settlers	102
XI.	A Game of Bluff	112
XII.	Keeping House for my Companions	124
XIII.	About Deer Shooting	135
XIV.	A Ride on a Deer's Back in the Lake	150
XV.	"I'll teach them how to shoot Deer"	164
XVI.	A Providential Dream	171
XVII.	"Did you ever know what it is to be blind? I have"	183
XVIII.	A Night on the Lake in a Snowstorm	191
XIX.	About Mines, &c	195
XX.	Lost in the Woods	210

XXI.	Among the Wolves	222
XXII.	"A Pretty Tall Snake Story"	240
XXIII.	About Bruin	249
XXIV.	More about Bruin	258
XXV.	The Breaking-up of the Ice	271
	A Backwoods Schoolmaster of the Olden Time	283
XXVI.	Jams	301
XXVII.	Sandy C—	316
XXVIII.	A Carnival in a River-side Shebeen	329
XXIX.	Shooting the Rapids and Slides of the Grand River	339
XXX.	Settling up in Quebec	347

SHANTY, FOREST AND RIVER LIFE.

CHAPTER I.

Reminiscences. Reflections.

I REMEMBER well the first gun I ever possessed, and that was many, many years ago. I was a youngster of about twelve, and the piece was proportionate in size to my years. It was a little old-fashioned thing, no more than three feet long, stock, barrel and all. I found it in the garret of one of my father's parishioners, to whom I was paying a visit at the time in company with my mother.

Long Peter—for so our host was called, to distinguish him from several others of the same name and clan in the settlement—was as long-headed as he was long-bodied, and as big in heart as he was in frame. I had always been a great favorite with him, and in my boyish conceit had the idea that I could wheedle almost anything out of him that was at all in reason. So as soon as my eyes lit on the gun I set my heart on it, and that gun I was bound to have. My importunities finally prevailed over Peter's reluctance to entrust me with it, and after making me promise not to tell my mother, and solemnly cautioning me to be careful in using it, he promised me the loan of it for an indefinite period.

As it was impossible to take the gun with me that day in the buggy with my mother, I tramped out the three miles to Peter's place early the next morning; and as I marched home with it on my shoulder I shall never forget the feelings of intense gratification and pride which filled my heart, and how I revelled in the anticipations of coming sport and slaughter among the squirrels and pigeons.

I have often wondered how I escaped blowing my brains out with that gun. It had seen so much duty in its day, and experienced such rough usage, that it was almost burned through at the breech. Every time I fired a little puff of smoke would come out through a small hole just below the nipple, and why it didn't burst in my hands has been a puzzle to me ever since. However, there was a grain of caution in me, even at that early age, and when I noticed this peculiarity about the breech, I resolved to test the piece before I would have anything more to do with it. So I put in a charge of powder four times as large as the ordinary measure, and fastened the gun firmly to a post in the barn-yard; then tying a string about fifty feet long to the trigger, and holding the other end, I ensconced myself in the roothouse, feeling assured that if it stood that charge it would be quite safe for ordinary practice. The report which followed my pull of the string was something tremendous, but I was delighted beyond measure, when I emerged from my covert, to find that the little gun had stood the test nobly, and was quite uninjured, though a larger column of smoke than usual came pouring out of that ominous hole.

After this I took great satisfaction out of "Birdie," as I fondly christened my tiny firearm; and after school-hours, in the long summer evenings, I had many a joyous ramble over the hills, and through the woods; and many a squirrel and pigeon and partridge became a trophy of its prowess.

From the possession of that piece I date my love of the woods, and of Nature in all her free, wild, and grand simplicity. And as the years have rolled on, and I have come to man's estate, and entered upon the stern duties of life, this love has never waned—but seems rather upon occasion at least to grow with my years—and I fervently hope that it never will while life lasts. But in justice to myself I must say that I have never allowed it to interfere with or hinder real work and duty; but when legitimate holiday comes, as come it should at least once a year to every professional man, then, instead of dawdling it away by the seaside, or at fashionable watering-places, with their senseless fripperies, and inane round of unmeaning and sensational amusements—a rehash, in fact, of city and artificial life—I love

> " To fold my tent, like the Arabs,
> And silently steal away "

to the quiet solitudes of nature, where, from lake and river, mountain and forest I draw that pure, healthy, and bracing excitement, both of body and mind, which constitutes the true rest of life, and the only genuine relaxation from overstrained mental and physical work, and at the same time the best invigorator for a fresh entry into the routine activities of life's duties. "A sound mind in a sound body" is one of the wisest maxims ever uttered by either Christian or Pagan philosopher. I care not how great a man's mental capacity may be, he never will fulfil the full complement of his work, if his body is weak and ailing. No doubt, by a tremendous exertion of will-power, his mind may rise superior to bodily infirmity, and work on passively and doggedly, and even produce magnificent results, as is grandly illustrated in the history of Dr. Johnston, Carlyle, Kepler and some others whose names are illustrious in the honor-roll of life's work. But these exceptional cases only falsely beg the question. For there is not a doubt that, if these same men had enjoyed vigorous health, free, full, and normal circulation of the blood, easy and natural respiration, and buoyant, elastic, physical spirits—in a word, a sound body, they would have accomplished double the work they did.

It is fearful to think how the intellectual energies of many of our best educated men in any direction you choose to look at, in science, theology, literature, politics, or business, are crippled, actually shorn of half their practical ability by neglecting or despising the claims of the body. This is very often the result of a foolish, false pride, or of abject moral cowardice.

There are many professional men who deem it "infra dignitatem" to take that physical exercise which will insure them vigorous, exuberant health, no matter how innocent or enjoyable these exercises may be. They fancy that it lowers their professional status to take an oar in hand, a rifle on their arm, or a pack on their shoulders, and tramp off to the wild woods, or other free domains of grand old Dame Nature, there to reap the purest, balmiest, most healthful of all life's enjoyments. If they do extend any favor to "that sort of thing" it is with a *dilettante* kind of air, a species of simpering patronage, which is as silly as it is uncalled for. I pity these men from the bottom of my heart. They know not how they are robbing themselves of what mainly constitutes true life in its actuality, longevity, and enjoyment.

But there is another class of professional men whom I despise with all my heart, and that is those who, through fear of public opinion, or slavish cringing to popular prejudice, are afraid to indulge in those harmless and healthy recreations which nature demands for the proper and adequate performance of life's work and duty. They perversely choose to live on, in a bilious, dyspeptic, abnormal condition of body and mind; misperforming solemn duty in a slipshod, treadmill, perfunctory sort of manner—in a word, are practical failures in respect to the potential abilities, the educational attainments, and all the other favorable surroundings with which a kind Providence has blessed them. And all because they have not the courage of their convictions, and are afraid to act up to the honest, sound, natural promptings of their own judgment and conscience.

En passant, it is pitiable to see how many of those

who ought to lead public opinion—to mould, regulate and elevate it—are led by it; instead of governing, which is their "divine right," in virtue of their position and attainments, they are the governed—they are slaves where they ought to be masters. This cringing and fawning after popular favor, this abnegation of what is truly noble and dignified in man's moral, intellectual and physical status, is one of the most odious and contemptible phases in all the multiform evolutions of human nature.

In nothing is this more strikingly shewn than in **this** question **of physical** recreation and exercise—though within these last few years there are many professional men of all grades who are adopting a more common-sense view of the matter. Instead of spending their two months' holidays in crowded, fashionable haunts, they are pitching their tents on some of the glorious islands of the St. Lawrence, in the more retired solitudes of our inland lakes, or in the depths of our sublime and pathless forests. Here, especially during the hot summer months, **they** and their families **can spend a most** delightful time. In fishing, canoeing, swimming, roughing it generally in the open, breezy, bracing air, with the pleasant accompaniments of light reading and family sociability, they quickly recuperate their overstrained energies, and brace themselves for another campaign on the dusty treadmill of town or city life.

I hold that such a life, for a season, above all others, gives genuine tone and power to the whole system, both mental and physical. Instead of demoralizing and unfitting for even the most serious and responsible duties, it rather nerves and braces for discharging them with redoubled zeal, energy and success. We would then have truer men, better preachers, sounder Christians, and a happier class generally of professional men, because a healthier, more clear-sighted and pure-hearted one.

Let me not be misunderstood in these reflections. I do not mean them as an apology or defence for my own likings and doings in this direction. By no means. On the contrary, I feel that the church and society in general are greatly obligated to me for bringing this question fairly and squarely before them; and I know that it meets with a hearty response in the minds of all right-discerning and good-sense people, if they only had the courage and honesty to admit it.

In one of the vicissitudes of my professional life I found myself, in the Fall of 188—, thrown upon my oars, and for some months to come practically my own master, as far as active duty was concerned.

At this juncture my friend C——, who always turns up at my right elbow in most opportune style, wrote me most urgently to pay a visit to his shanties on the Madawasca, and head waters of the Clyde, telling me to "make myself at home there, and stay as long as I pleased, months, years, a century if I chose." He gave me, at the same time, a letter to his general manager, the gist of which was that he was to see that "Mr. F. was treated in every way the same as if it were himself."

Without hesitation I accepted his kind invitation, and made my arrangements accordingly.

My friend Costen, in his usual, efficient manner, fitted me out with all needful hunting and camping accoutrements; and with an abundant supply of books, clothes and all necessary comforts, I found myself, after a few days, *en route*, in great glee of heart, for the backwoods.

CHAPTER II.

Manahan's Shanty and Surroundings.

HAD no occasion, on this trip to the backwoods, to drive four days through the piny wilderness, before reaching my destination.

My journey this time was a very simple and prosaic affair. The K. and P. R. would carry me within seven miles of C.'s nearest shanty.

So, on the evening of the second day after leaving home, I found myself "rubbing" along on the last stage of the road between Mississippi station and the terminus, which rejoices under the appropriate name of Iron City. It is in the immediate vicinity of most valuable iron mines, and in fact lies at the base of a mighty hill, which is commonly supposed, especially by the credulous in these matters, to be one solid mass of magnetic ore.

In due time next day, I arrived at my destination—Manahan's shanty,—and received a cordial and hearty welcome from my old friend and school-fellow, the foreman.

I felt myself at once thoroughly at home, **and surrounded** by many old friends. Some of these were sons of **my** father's old parishioners, whom I had known when a boy. Others, and not a few, had been with me as canoemen and hunters in former expeditions to the backwoods. Though it was some years since I had been in this country, yet they all remembered me, and from one and all I received an iron grip of the hand, which said better than words how glad they were to see me. Each one had some stirring incident, or old pleasant reminiscence to recall. "Do you remember the time Mr. F., etc., etc.," was the usual introduction to a long and friendly talk. How pleasant it is in again meeting with former associates to feel that there are no old heart-burnings existing still between you. **Many** a "tiff" and hot row I had had with some of these fellows over some trifling matter concerning **cámp or** hunt, but all seemed now forgotten, and **they** were as ready as ever to help and befriend me.

As for myself, as I sat that night before the great fire, I felt a thrill of delight at being once more among these sturdy, manly, warm-hearted sons of the forest. Take them all in all I love the shanty-men. There is more of true manliness, of genuine unsophisticated, right-heartedness among them than in any class of men I ever associated with.

Manahan's shanty is situated in a wild, rough country of rocky hills, tangled swamp and boggy marshes. In common with the larger portion of the Ottawa Valley, the district is totally unfit for cultivation. The few settlers who farm the land depend entirely upon the lumber business for their bare subsistence. Not only does it afford a ready and high market for the scanty produce of their farms—consisting almost solely of oats and hay (for not one in ten ever has a bushel of wheat to sell in a year),—but both men and horses obtain steady employment during the winter in the shanties. With all the available resources which they can possibly command, the great majority of them are a poor, hard-working, hand-to-mouth class of people.

I often wonder what induced sensible people, with their eyes open, to settle in this part of the country with the view of making a living by farming.

When the lumber business dies out, which it must of necessity do before many years, this section must in a large measure become depopulated, for the land cannot and never will be able to support any but the scantiest population. However we have great faith in the development of the mineral resources of the country; and if capital and enterprise are only fairly evoked in this direction, there will always be a fair market for the surplus products of the land, and also for the labor of men and horses.

In so speaking I do not ignore the fact that there are some farmers who, through superior intelligence, indefatigable industry and rigid economy, have done fairly well—in fact, may be called well-to-do farmers, but, emphatically, they are "few and very far between." The great proportion, no doubt three-fourths of those who profess to till the soil, do not and cannot live by it. If, then, the mining interest will not take the place of lumber business, these people must either starve or leave.

What adds to the wild and sterile appearance of this district are the terrible ravages of the fire-fiend, vast tracts of the most valuable timber sections have again and again been devastated by this scourge. (Of this, however, and also of the mineral resources of the country, I shall treat more fully in subsequent chapters.) Consequently, for miles in every direction, the country is diversified, though certainly not beautified, by dead, burnt pineries. The tall black trunks of these mighty giants of the forest, denuded of their branches, tower upwards to a great height, and present a weird, desolate landscape to the view. In backwoods parlance they are called "rampikes," and make you think of the crowbars which the Titans may have used to pry up the rocks, with which they tried to pelt Jupiter out of Heaven.

Notwithstanding the ravages of the fire, however, one is astonished at the vast amount of virgin forest which still remains, and the immense number of fine logs and square timber that is being taken out.

C—— has five shanties in active operation within a radius of four miles. These shanties are distinguished by the names of their respective foremen, viz., Monahan's, where my headquarters are, Larocque's, Rice's, Craig's, and Stoughton's. In each of these a full complement of men, between thirty and forty, are busy at work, felling, scoring, hewing, sawing and drawing unto the ice.

C—— expects to take out this season 60,000 logs, and a large raft of square timber. He has also on these limits an immense quantity of most valuable oak, birch, basswood, cedar, ash, rock-elm, and, perhaps best of all, bird's eye and curly maple. He is building a large steam saw mill in the very heart of those invaluable woods, by which he intends to utilize them to the very last tree.

It is a singular spectacle to see this great work going on in the depths of the wilderness, for so it yet practically is, and awakens unbounded astonishment in the eyes of the surrounding *habitans*. But that great civilizer, the railway, has come, and is breaking down and casting up the highways of backwoods thought and life. In another year or two there will be no backwoods here, and its lovers will have to go further back for a camp or a home.

By next July the road is expected to be built within half a mile of the mill, with which it will be connected by a switch. It was of course with this probability in view that C—— decided to build the mill, otherwise he might as well have thrown his money into the fire, because there was no possibility of getting his lumber out when sawn except by a railway. The building of the mill itself is a great undertaking, and is regarded by many wise and other heads as chimerical in the extreme. At the very outset the blasting of the rock in order to secure a solid foundation on which to rest the gangways is a herculean task, and involves an immense expenditure of money, dynamite and labor.

The noise and dust that these fellows kick up in their work is something terrific. When half a dozen blasts go off at once, as frequently happens, you would fancy two or three volcanoes and earthquakes had burst out simultaneously. But Browne, the foreman, is an expert and pushing fellow, and expects, as he says, to have the whole rock cleared out of that "in less than no time."

C——'s idea in building this mill is an exceedingly far-seeing and long-headed one, and, as far as human prescience and calculation can determine, an exceedingly profitable one. He purposes running the mill all the year round. In the summer he will cut nothing but pine, of which, notwithstanding the fires, he has still sufficient to last for several years. During the winter season he will saw nothing but the hard woods, for the simple reason that these woods cannot be taken out during the summer, as they will not float in the streams, but, as they are in the vicinity of the mill, they can be drawn direct to it on the snow-roads, just when they are cut, and the boards by the railroad shipped direct to market. The enterprise is a thoroughly sound one. Between soft and hard woods he has an abundant supply for ten years to come, and by that time the mill will have paid itself many times over, and he can afford to let it go to decay and ruin if it likes, for all he cares.*

Monahan's shanty, built under his own supervision, is a capital specimen, of its kind, of backwoods architecture. It is warm, roomy, lightsome, and "doesn't smoke." Smoke is the pest of the shantyman's domicile. It requires very considerable mechanical ingenuity, and practical experience, so to construct the camboose and the opening in the roof immediately above it, with its log chimney of few or many feet in height, that the smoke may escape

---

* Since the above was written C's—— plans and expectations have been fully realized. The railroad has been built to the mill, and is in regular running to a point three miles beyond it. The mill is finished, though at an enormous expense, and after many vexatious accidents and delays, and is now turning out its 60,000 feet a day. What a year ago was a thickety, marshy swamp is now a scene of lively, bustling activity. A village of over thirty houses has sprung up which rejoices in the apt name of Clyde Forks. The whole enterprise has proved a grand success, and is one of the most striking illustrations we have of what determination, combined with long-headedness and capital, can accomplish. C—— has struck the key-note in this direction, his uncle, Mr. B. C., one of the wealthiest lumber merchants of the Ottawa, is building a large steam mill on his limits, about ten miles further south on the line of railway, and others, I hear, are about to follow in the wake.

freely and fully. Even with the best and most *experimental* precautions there are few shanties but will smoke sometimes. It depends greatly upon the weather: when the atmosphere is damp, foggy and depressed it is often impossible to prevent it. Our shanty is one of the best in this respect I have ever been in; and in it, until I moved to the mill quarters, I spent a most comfortable and happy time.

Monahan's "gang" of forty men is a fair sample of the shanty *genus homo*; English, Scotch, Irish and French are its constituent elements, and among them are some splendid specimens of physical humanity.

Jim himself is a capital type of the shanty foreman. He is a tall, well proportioned, powerful man; with great push and energy of character. And, though he has all the "*brusqueness*" of manner which perhaps too much belongs to men of his position, yet he is greatly liked and respected by his men. He is always ready to grant a reasonable favor, and do a kind and generous action, and at the same time, both by example and rule, he endeavors to inculcate sobriety and good behavior among the men. He is an intelligent, well-educated man, and a most insatiable reader. He is

Menahan's Shanty.

always cribbing my books, if they are lying loose about, concerning which we have many a friendly tiff.

Shanty life would be monotonous in the extreme, were it not for the vigorous exercise in the open, bracing air, and the redundant health, with its natural accompaniment of high animal spirits, which is almost continually enjoyed.

Still the men have their amusements: at night when supper is over, it is a cheery sight to see them round the roaring fire, in the full enjoyment of that sweetest of all rest which follows after hard, lengthy, and healthy labor in a bright, keen atmosphere, surcharged with ozone and oxygen, and impregnated with the balmy odors of the pine, balsam, spruce and tamarac.

Cards, chequers, reading if they have books—and they always have where I am—an occasional dance, song and story, all accompanied by the merry strains of the fiddle, and, better than all, a *camaraderie* which pervades the whole—make the long winter evenings pass quickly and pleasantly, until it is time to turn in under the warm blankets, to sleep that sweet, sound and refreshing slumber, which only strong men in the redundance of health and animal life, without care or thought of the morrow, can obtain and realize.

CHAPTER III.

Shanty Government.

IN a community of men, so isolated and far removed from the ordinary restraints of social and judicial influence, it may be supposed that absolute lawlessness, and reckless independence will reign supreme, that each man of these hardy, rough-and-ready sons of the forest will think and act as if he were a law to himself. But such is very far from being the case. There is government and discipline in shanty life, just as pronounced and strictly carried out as in the most exemplary and well-regulated village, town, or city corporation of the Dominion.

"If you think you can do as you like in this shanty," I once heard a foreman say to a blustering green-hand, "you make a d——l of a mistake."

The remark struck me at the time, as I have no doubt it does you, Reader, as very expressive, but it is, in fact, the clue to the whole question. It is just on this point that the judicious and successful lumber merchant shews very conspicuously his sagacity and knowledge of his business. He knows that one of the prime essentials for carrying on a successful season's work is securing the right stamp of men for foremen. Hence he exercises all his caution and experience in the selection of these men.

And they, on the other hand, are given very plainly to understand the obligations and responsibilities they assume when they undertake the position. It is not merely that they must be men of experience in the woods—men who know *where*, and *how*, to build a shanty on a spot in the midst of the best and largest quantity of timber in the limit, with the shortest " draw " to the nearest river; and who know experimentally every detail of the business from " cook's-mate " up to hewer; but, above all this and chiefly, they must know how to *govern men*. To hold their own with the most refractory and self-opinionated—to insist upon every man doing as he is told, and fulfilling his full and fair quota of work, and conducting himself in a quiet and orderly way in the shanty; and at the same time to exercise great caution not to be too arbitrary with, or abuse them.

These conditions and mutual obligations are generally very clearly understood between foreman and men, and, as a rule, there is very little disturbance of the peace, or absence of harmony in the general working of both inside and out-door shanty life.

I know, however, of some notable exceptions, which I cannot do better than narrate, as thoroughly illustrative of some very interesting and characteristic phases of the question.

They occurred in the shanties of the lumbering concern of my friend C——, on the upper waters of the Black River. In this far remote and isolated region of the Upper Ottawa, the discipline of the shanty must be exercised with peculiar tact and judgment by the foreman. If men are discharged, or leave of their own accord, it may be some weeks before they can be replaced, and, consequently, the business of the concern may be seriously damaged. So, in order to get the full amount of work out of the men, and at the same time keep them at it, the foreman must have all his wits about him in managing them.

Now it happened that in one of my friend's shanties there were some refractory fellows who would not pull in the traces, especially two, who were the chief agents in these seditious movements, and whose evil influence was rapidly inoculating the whole shanty with their pernicious sentiments. Without setting the foreman openly at defiance, they would shirk work, or only half do it, and also in many a tricky way hinder the other well-disposed and industrious men from doing their work. The foreman was completely at his wit's ends how to manage them. He did not want to discharge them, and he was afraid to take the law in his own hands, for they were lusty, powerful fellows, and might turn Turk on him.

In these straits my friend, who is a famous strategist in such affairs, bethought him of a plan by which he might remedy the evil.

He had in his employment at the time another foreman who was a man of a very different stamp from the one I have just referred to. Larry, for that was his name, was a notorious character. He was a man of wonderful strength and agility, and a perfect fiend in fighting when roused or in liquor, though ordinarily he was of a quiet, inoffensive disposition, and a most faithful, expert workman. In many ways C—— looked upon him as one of the best foremen he ever had in his employment.

"Larry," said he, "you must take in hand these two rascals."

"Just send them to me," replied Larry, "and I'll take care of them."

So the very next day the two confederates who were causing all the trouble in the other shanty, were ordered, greatly to their surprise, to go to work in Larry's shanty, and their place was supplied by two of his best and most peaceful men.

Everything went off well for a day or two, until Larry thought he saw symptoms of the two fellows beginning at their old tricks, and, as he had fully arranged in his own mind, he at once resolved to put in operation his plan for checking it,—and, perhaps, this plan was as unique and interpenetrative of human nature as has been adopted from the days of Solomon down.

While the men were smoking their usual post-prandial pipe, in the interval always allowed before proceeding to work, Larry suddenly called out, "Come, boys, let's have a little fun, let us have a fight before we go to work." And naming the two conspirators in all the shanty difficulties, he told them to go out in front of the shanty, and set to with each other—"just for the sake of fun," said the knowing dog, "to see which is the best man."

The two fellows at first demurred, but Larry insisted, and with such a look in his eye, and tone of voice, that they thought it better to obey, and, stripping off, and, in the midst of the whole turned-out shanty, at it they went, apparently in great good-humor. But Larry knew well enough what would follow. From fun they got into earnest, from being in earnest they became infuriated, and gave each other such a fearful mauling that they were disabled for work for the rest of the day.

But the evil was cured, and the two men and all other evil-disposed fellows in both shanties did their work, and kept fully up to the mark for the rest of the season.

Never was there an expedient for gaining an end more replete with human craft and practical acquaintance with the weaknesses of a vanity-stricken heart, in conjunction with the surroundings, than this. If Larry had been educated and gone into politics, and had a consciousness of his own abilities, and assurance in proportion, he might have been prime minister of the nation.

But I have another incident to tell about Larry which is illustrative of another phase of shanty discipline, and, though quite in keeping with his well-known character as a "fighter,"—for we cannot call him a pugilist—is yet happily almost now an unknown occurrence.

Two men, for some cause, whether justifiable or not--nobody knows better than themselves--deserted.

from Larry's shanty, and started for the settlements. Larry, however, had his own opinion on the subject, and, being in one of his aroused humors, determined to make an example of the fellows. Harnessing his horse and cutter (there happened to be one belonging to the concern in the stable at the time), he drove rapidly in the direction the men had taken, and overtook them as they were taking their dinner, in a shanty about twenty miles away.

Larry was decidedly in a baddish sort of humor that day. After eating his own dinner, and talking quietly all the time to the two men, he told them to go back to their work. Upon their flatly refusing to do so, he fell upon them, and gave them a most unmerciful beating, and then, kicking them out into the road, he ordered them to go ahead, and actually drove them like cattle in front of his horse, all the way back to the shanty. Needless to say there was no further attempt at desertion that winter, either on their part, or on that of any of the rest of the men.

There is rather a new phase of shanty government being developed within the last few years, and that is the appointment of general managers over the business. Those lumber-merchants who carry on an extensive business, say of three or more shanties, and perhaps have other large interests to attend to, are now in the habit of appointing a "manager" who has full oversight and charge of all the foremen and men, and is directly responsible to the proprietors for the general "running" of the concern. Those gentlemen, however, are very chary how they interfere between the foreman and his men; though if any difficulty does arise they are the referees who arbitrate upon it.

The "manager" of C—'s business in this place is a gentleman who is widely known throughout Canada and the North-west, in connection with lumber matters. He is best known in Central Canada by the name of "Big Duncan," and if ever a man merited the epithet it is certainly he.

He is a modern Goliath, a veritable Anak. In his stocking feet he towers aloft to the altitude of six feet two, and carries with ease his weight of seventeen stone. Duncan is considerable of a wag in his way, and as inveterate a practical joker as any schoolboy that ever lived. In common with all managers he has his difficulties in the government of the large force of men which are under his command; but he never fails to have his joke, even when exercising the most severe discipline. One morning he came in to where I was sitting writing, and in his deep-measured tones, and with a countenance as grave and solemn as that of a county judge, he said, " Mr. F— I have just effected a dissolution of partnership in this concern. There are three fellows in Joe's shanty who have been so long in this family that they fancy they are members of the firm, and can come and go, and do as they please; so this morning I told them they could go home if they liked, and stay there if they liked, but never show their faces here again."

Of course, the fact that they can discharge men when they please, without detriment to the business —being so near the settlements that they can quickly replace them—gives the manager and foreman the whip-hand over the men in maintaining the order and general efficiency of the shanty.

Be this as it may, however, I never wish to live in a more orderly, peaceful and harmonious community than that which I have seen in shanty life. The general tone of it is not only kind and friendly, but brotherly in the highest degree. It is more like a united and well-dispositioned family than an "*omnium gatherum*" of strong, rough men, of all ages, nationalities and religions,

CHAPTER IV.

"I'll roast the Devil out of you."

A GREAT mistake is entertained by many people regarding the general character of shantymen: they are commonly looked upon as a wild harum-scarum class of men who have no right sense of the decencies and proprieties of ordinary respectable life, who when they go to the woods leave behind them their good manners and morals, along with their Sunday clothes. That the shanty itself is a city of refuge for the abandoned and profligate of the earth, and resounds continually with oaths and profanities of the vilest nature is a common error.

Hence it is that many a pious mother and father regard with trembling apprehension the idea of their young son, who perhaps is the main breadwinner of the family, going to spend the long winter months with some lumbering concern in the depths of the forest. And yet he must go. It would never do to remain all winter at home in comparative idleness. The greater part of the farm work is done for the year, and the team and young able-bodied man must not live upon the scanty returns of perhaps a poor harvest, while good wages and sumptuous living for man and beast are at his command. The old father, and perhaps a younger brother or sister, are quite sufficient to tend the cattle, chop the firewood, and do all the other little "chores" about the place until springtime comes again. So with many a misgiving they allow him to go, with team and "bobsleigh" all in "tiptop" order, probably not to return until the season's work is over.

Now there is no doubt that this low estimate of character is tolerably correct as applied to the average shantyman of many years ago. But it does not hold true now in any sense whatsoever. A great change for the better has been wrought in the character and conduct of these men. I don't believe that, take them as a whole, there is a more sober, orderly, and well-behaved class of laboring men in the world than our backwoods and river lumbering men. To compare them with the working men of our towns and cities, such as ship laborers, canal or railroad navvies, or laborers generally on our large public works, would be, I consider, an atrocious libel upon them—a comparison not to be entertained for a moment. This is the unanimous testimony of all the competent authorities I have consulted on the matter, and, as far as my own experience of twenty years goes, I *know* it to be the case.

Swearing is at a discount among them. Lewd conversation and songs are not tolerated. Liquor is not allowed in, or near the shanty. And, as we shall see further on, they welcome and listen with great attention and respect to the preaching of the Gospel.

I account for this great change in the morals and habits of this class on two grounds:

First, there is a different class seeking work and being engaged by the employers from what used to be. A few years ago the great bulk of the men were hired at Ottawa and Quebec, and were principally French Canadians, of the lowest class. Now, since the sawn lumber business has assumed such large proportions, the drive on the river is comparatively short, generally over by the first of June, consequently a much larger number of the farmers' sons in the vicinity of the works are seeking employment, as they generally can get home in time for sowing the crop; and as they are a much more steady and reliable class, and just as able-bodied and skilful workmen, they are more readily engaged than any others. The number of men who engage in the fall to go through to Quebec is but a fraction of what it used to be, and the number of French Canadians who work in the woods is now reduced to a minimum.

Hence the *personnel* of the shanty is greatly changed, and that vastly for the better, within the last few years.

Another reason, and one that is a mighty factor in this improved state of things, is that the foremen, as a rule, are exerting themselves more strongly in favor of sobriety and morality. The foremen themselves are a better class of men. The old bullying, brute-force principle of governing is now almost entirely done away with. The merchants now endeavor to engage foremen who are men of intelligence, fair education, and of tried and proved ability. They find it pays best in every way—more and better work is done. The wheels of the machine—and there is none more complicated and requiring more business engineering than it—run more smoothly, and both employers and employés find it to be for their mutual comfort and advantage.

A foreman now-a-days never thinks of taking a handspike and knocking a man down if he neglects his duty, or is in any way refractory. If the man will not listen to remonstrance or reproof, he orders the clerk to "give him his time," and then quietly tells him to leave. The dread of this has a far more powerful effect upon the men in keeping them up to the mark than handspikes or fisticuffs.

To be sure, there is not much of what we call demonstrative piety among them, either as foremen or employés. As a class they are reticent and reserved as to emotional display in any direction, and no doubt specially so in religious matters. In this respect, they greatly resemble soldiers of the regular forces. But, where it is displayed, it is of a very pronounced and decided kind, and no cant or humbug about it.

I have in my mind's-eye at this moment a gentleman widely known in the lumbering country, Mr. R—, commonly called Bob R—. Bob was highly respected by all who know him for his kindly disposition, sterling integrity, and sound, practical sense. He was a deacon, and an active and liberal supporter of his church. He had had many vicissitudes of fortune in the lumbering business, but at the time of his death, some three years since, was comparatively wealthy. Bob was a very strict disciplinarian among his men in religious matters. He would allow no swearing nor card-playing in his shanties, at least while he was present to prevent it, though in this latter particular I think he was strict over much. I see no harm in the men, especially those who can't read, whiling away the long winter's evening in a game of euchre or forty-five, which are the favorite, in fact the only games, with shanty-men; and particularly so when there is no gambling or drinking connected with it. Be this as it may, Bob would tolerate neither the one nor the other, as the following incident very emphatically shows.

On a certain occasion, when he was visiting one of his shanties, one of the men, a big Frenchman, resolved to assert his independence and defiance of Bob on these points. He was one of those bullying blustering fellows that you often meet with among these men, who mistake their bluster for courage and high spirit, but are simply a pest and a nuisance in the shanty. This man, in spite of Bob's frowns and rebukes, would persist in his profane and rebellious course, until Bob's righteous soul was stirred within him.

The men looked curiously on. A scene was evidently impending. Now, our friend was a very large and heavily built man, and though rather awkward in his movements, was possessed of great physical vigor, and when thoroughly roused—which was very seldom the case, as he was a man of great and long-suffering good-nature—was an ugly and formidable customer to deal with. Bob began to see that the man was continuing his profanities just for the purpose of annoying and riling him. When this impression dawned upon, and became a conviction within him, then a terrible storm of righteous indignation burst upon his soul, and suddenly rising he laid violent hands upon the bully. For a time he seemed endued with the strength of ten men, and soon laid the man *hors de combat*. But his holy wrath was not appeased with this victory: seizing the man with one hand by the back of the neck and with the other by the seat of his unmentionables he held him bodily over the fire of the *camboose*, thundering at the same time in his ears " I'll roast the devil out of you." The fellow roared and begged for mercy, and managing to escape out of his clutches, he bolted out of the door, and would not return to the shanty while Bob remained.

Now decisive action of this kind produces a most salutary effect in the direction we indicated upon men of this stamp. It is worth a dozen sermons. In fact, it is the only effectual way of dealing with that class of which this Frenchman was a type. And the general effect is not only good, but is highly applauded by the great bulk of the men. They like the pluck of the thing, and the honesty of the " boss " to his creed. It shows them that his religion is not a mere profession, but a conviction, a rule of practice as well as of faith. An incident of this kind, apart altogether from the moral side of it, meets with a great deal of sympathy and commendation from those rough and ready, open-hearted fellows. It is certain to become widely known, and as it is discussed in all its bearings round the *camboose*, you will find that the almost unanimous verdict is in favor, not only of the action itself, but also of the principle which underlies it.

We believe that the good moral influence of that roasting is felt among shantymen to this day throughout that whole section of the Ottawa Valley.

CHAPTER V.

A Merry Old Cook.

ONE of the most important personages about the shanty is the cook. If you wish to enjoy yourself, and have some fair measure of comfort, you must keep on good terms with him. It will never do to fall out with the cook; you may as well take up your blankets and walk. In many ways he is a more consequential individual than the foreman himself. In fact he looks after and has a voice in every department of the internal economy of the shanty. He tells you where you must sleep, in what corner you must stow your bag, and on what peg you are to hang your socks, moccasins and clothes.

He is the oracle of the establishment, and his opinion is consulted by every one connected with it. Not only by the magic power of good cooking, but by his general disposition and temper, he exerts an influence in the shanty which greatly affects its general peace and comfort. Hence the employer selects the cook with great care, and gives him the highest wages, often double what an ordinary working man can command.

And you would be amazed at the general excellence of the cooking that is done by these fellows. Where will you find such bread as is made in their immense pots, buried in and covered over by the hot ashes at the end of the *camboose?* Not a particle of the strength and fine flavor of the flour is lost by evaporation, as in the case of a stove or open oven: it is all condensed in the bread. Then it is strong and firm, and yet—and this is the mystery to me—it is light and porous as that of any first-class housewife's.

And what shall we say about the beans? They are simply *par excellence.* They are baked in the same kind of pot as the bread, the lid being hermetically sealed to the rim by dough, and then buried in the hot ashes. The beans are first thoroughly sifted, washed and boiled; and then large slices of fat pork mixed with them. The pot is then placed in its deep bed of hot ashes, and, as in the case of the bread, not a breath of steam or of the essence of the bean allowed to escape. The fat pork becoming dissolved by the heat, and of course neither fried nor boiled as in other processes, becomes amalgamated with the beans, and when the whole is considered sufficiently cooked, a mess is ready, which, for succulency of flavor and savory richness of nutrition, will completely throw into the shade the famous pottage for which Esau bartered his birthright.

It is strong food, of course, the very strongest, I believe, in the world. A person who is accustomed to the ordinary dishes of domestic cooking must be cautious how he attacks it at first. If he takes too heavy an allowance, as he is strongly tempted to do on account of its savoriness, he will be very likely to throw his stomach into convulsions. But it is the grandest food in the world for shantymen, whose vigorous open-air exercise in the keen oxygenated atmosphere enables them to digest food which would upset and demoralize the stomach of a town or city man.

Beans have entirely superseded peas, and are now one of the staple articles of shanty diet. There is a staying power in them which I believe is possessed by no other food, that is, when prepared in the way I describe. I have often taken a large tin plate-full in the morning, and then tramped the whole day through the woods, till after dark, and yet felt no pressing sensation of hunger or fatigue.

To my mind it is the best kind of food that could be used in our Arctic expeditions. In proportion to its nutritive power its bulk weight is the most portable in the world. Five quarts of beans will make a good meal for forty men, of course along with tea and bread or hard-tack. No doubt it would be impracticable to prepare beans in the proper way on the sleighing parties; but the same purpose would be served by cooking a large quantity on the ship, and allowing the conglomerated mess to freeze into a solid mass, and then chop off and warm up as occasion required. I believe it would be a better food than pemmican, and, while most palatable to the men, there would not be a taint of scurvy in a barrel of it; in fact, it would be rather a preventive to the dire scourge of the north.

I think the British and American governments should give me a vote of thanks for the suggestions I have thrown out on this bean question, and utilize them in their proposed international expedition to the polar regions.

There is a great improvement now-a-days, not only in the *cuisine*, but also in the *materiel*—the food itself provided for the shantymen. Years ago pork, tea and bread were the sole food of the men, and sometimes not too much of that, nor of the best quality either. In nothing in shanty life is there a greater change noticeable than in this matter. Now, not only is the **food** superabundant, but **also of the most** varied and best quality. Compared to the other laboring classes, our shantymen fare sumptuously every day. What do you think of such a bill of fare as this, which constitutes the daily routine of my friend C—'s *menu:* Mess pork, *fresh* beef, bread, tea, dried apples stewed, **syrup,** beans, potatoes, sugar, often butter, *fish?* What laboring **men in the** world have such living as this, and what more, or, better could **the heart of a strong** healthy working man possibly **desire?**

At first sight it might appear that this great change for the better in shanty diet would involve a largely increased expenditure. But when we look into the matter closely, we **shall** find that **this is not** the case. Pork, tea, bread, **which** constituted **the staple articles of diet under the old regime, are the most expensive** of all **foods, and of course, having nothing** else, much larger quantities were consumed **by the men than at present,** when these **are supplemented by** potatoes, fish, &c., which in comparison are greatly cheaper. **In fact, this varied and** superior **diet** is, cent per **cent,** cheaper **actually than** the old unvaried **shanty fare.** But, **not only so, but** it is infinitely healthier **for the men, and** more and better work **can be done on** it than formerly.

But let us get back, as the title of this chapter intimates, to the cook himself, his *personnel*, &c. As can easily be understood, this gentleman, from his functions and surroundings, is often a *character*, one indeed well worthy of study and curious interest. I have in my mind's-eye many such with whom I have been well acquainted, and whom I count among my best friends, and of whom I have many pleasant and grateful remembrances—no doubt influenced thereto by a leaning to my own personal comfort and enjoyment, for I honestly confess to a weakness in the cookery direction.

Prominent among these stand out old Ned C——. I can never think of him without having recalled to my mind our school-boy rhyme of "King Cole," a travesty upon which will shape itself in my mind,

> "Old cook Ned, was a merry old cook,
> And a merry old cook was he;
> He rattled his pans, and swore by the book,
> And danced right merrily."

Ned was a little wizen-faced, crooked-mouthed, fiery-eyed old Frenchman. His countenance at times would assume a queer, comical, rat-like kind of seriousness, out of which his keen little eyes would leer at you with a droll, malicious devilment.

He was the best dancer I ever saw in the back-

A Merry Old Cook.

woods, and that is saying a good deal of a class noted for their agility and activity. When the day's work was over, the pans and dresser all scoured as bright as a shilling, and the lively strains of the fiddle were cheering up every heart, old Ned would sometimes be seized with a dancing humor, and then his antics round the *camboose* were simply prodigious. He had the floor all to himself, for no one presumed to rival or keep step with him in his complicated toeings and heelings, and agile bowings and scrapings. And there was a perfect contagion in the spirit of his dancing: it stimulated you for the time being into a feeling of emulation. You could not keep your legs and feet still. You felt as if you could leap over the *camboose,* and back again without any difficulty, though you might as well attempt to leap over the moon.

And yet there was no nonsense about old Ned. He was a perfect despot among his pots and pans. The puny little fellow would order about those great hulks of fellows as if they were children. "Go and wash your hands," you would hear him yell to some forgetful wight who had presumed to approach the steaming savory pot of pork and beans without having first performed this usual ablution.

These fellows, as a rule, are very cleanly in their

habits. Every man washes at the small hand-trough at the door as soon as he gets up, and every time he comes in for his meals. And if he neglects to do this, he is very quickly reminded of it by some authoritative individual like the cook.

Ned was very fond of me, and he showed his predilection in a highly satisfactory manner. When the men came in for their meals—and if you want to see good lusty, practical common-sense eating, now is the time for it—Ned would give me a queer knowing side-look, which said as plainly as words, "just wait a little, I've got something good for you." So, while the men were wondering at my patience and apparent indifference, I would be whetting my appetite with a little expectation of the coming "something good," and I was never disappointed. Many a royal "snack" the old fellow would thus prepare for me, which immensely comforted me in my shanty life. Merry, genial, kind-hearted old Ned—I'll never forget him while appetite and digestion remain, and I hope he will be long spared to give me many a toothsome "snack" yet.

In marked contrast to old Ned stood out young Alf, the "boy cook." Though only eighteen he is already a Goliath in stature, and will be, if he takes care of himself, a veritable Samson in strength. I have seen him stand on the shanty floor and without changing his position kick the roof with his foot—a test of physical power and suppleness of great authority with shantymen.

He is as pretty a youth as ever entered a shanty door. Notwithstanding the smoke and ashes and cinders of the *camboose*, in which he constantly moves, the bloom on his cheek is as fresh and peach-like as that of a girl of sixteen. His face is a continual sparkle of rosy, juvenile freshness, and does your soul good to look at it. If it were that of a girl you would be in love with it before your heart could throb twice. Young as he is, Alf has already attained high eminence in his profession, and is accounted by the men, with whom he is a general favorite, a "boss" cook.

There is many a hot dispute as to his proficiency in this line, compared to that of his brother George, who is the cook in our shanty. Of course I swear by George, though in truth there is little to choose between them, though George is several years older, and has the advantage of many years' experience; but both have an excellent repute, and command high wages.

George is a manly, good-looking, rather under-sized fellow, and though a famous fiddler, and a merry joker upon occasion, is yet in general of a staid, sedate, and self-repressed demeanor. He is even cross-grained and snappishly inclined at times, particularly when his liver gets out of gear, for cooking does not agree with his health, and he dislikes it, and nothing but the high wages keeps him at it, as he is a saving and money-loving dog. But he is married, and that I suppose accounts for all these latter peculiarities.

He is always dosing himself with patent nostrums, and is a fair sample of the gullibility of credulous humanity in this direction. I was greatly amused one night at a scene which took place in the shanty, which was about as striking an illustration of imitative credulity in human nature as I ever witnessed. George was greatly troubled with a sore throat, and was, in consequence, in one of his perverse humors. I felt sorry for him, for he was really suffering great distress, and offered him a dose of Thomas' Eclectric Oil, which is a capital specific for an acute attack of inflammation of the tonsils or bronchial tubes.

George most eagerly seized the teaspoon, and with great gravity prepared himself to take the medicine in prescribed form. The directions are to open the mouth as wide as possible, and, throwing the head well back, to retain the oil as long as you can in the throat, so that it may get well absorbed in the membranes before swallowing.

With great deliberation George seated himself on the *camboose*, and opening his mouth to its widest capacity, and throwing his head back almost to a right angle with his spine, he slowly imbibed the full quantity of the oil, intently and admiringly gazed at meanwhile by the whole shanty.

In my eager interest in watching the operation I found myself unconsciously imitating my patient's attitudes; checking myself with an inward chuckle at my goosiness, I looked round at the other fellows to see if they had noticed me, and to my astonished amusement there was every man-jack of them exhibiting the same phenomenon. Forty mouths were wide agape, forty heads were thrown backwards as far as they could go, and forty pairs of eyes were staring down the upturned noses, breathlessly and absorbingly fixed upon George. The thing struck me with such a sense of the ridiculous that my gravity was completely upset, and with a burst of outrageous laughter I broke the charm, and nearly choked poor George with the sudden gulp which he was compelled to take of the nauseous compound.

If my friend Notman could only have taken a photographic view of that circle of upturned, open-mouthed countenances, it would be one of the most striking and characteristic pictures in his gallery.

George, like many of his young compatriots, is smitten with the Manitoban fever, and is off to the land of the setting sun ; where I have not the least doubt that his honesty, and general practical ability will quickly gain for him a comfortable and prosperous career.

CHAPTER VI.

"My Home! My Home! My Home!"

ONE night as I was tramping weariedly shantywards I found to my surprise, and no little uneasiness, that it was considerably later than I had thought. In fact, night had overtaken me, and its dark shadows were coming down upon me before I realized it. I had had a long and heavy tramp that day over an exceedingly rough country, and felt almost fagged out, and for the last mile or so had been going quite leisurely, under the impression that I could easily reach the shanty before night. We read about the thief in the night, but on this occasion it was the night that was the culprit, and had stolen upon me most suddenly indeed.

Though I was not more than a mile from my destination still my course lay over burnt piny hills and dark thickety gullies, which were intersected in every direction by timber roads utterly indistinguishable in the dark from the true direction, except to one thoroughly familiar with them. This I certainly was not, as it was only the second time I had been over this route.

These timber roads are often exceedingly bewildering even to old experienced bush-rangers: they cross and recross each other at every conceivable angle and direction. They are a mazy labyrinth of road network, each one of which is a blind alley whose terminus is some " rollway " where a collection of logs or square timber has been made, ready to be drawn away by the teamsters. When the footsore traveller discovers his mistake he has nothing for it but simply to retrace his steps, and try another road, with perhaps the same disheartening result. And thus he may wander the whole night, and all the while keep within an area of a mile or less. The notorious " Will o' the Wisp " is not more tantalising and positively dangerous—that is on a cold night—than these timber roads;— all this I knew from bitter experience.

However, relief was just at hand : as the darkness fairly closed upon me I came to a cabin, which I know was just a mile from the shanty. I entered it, with the fervent prayer that the occupants would so press me to stay with them that I would be compelled to accept, as it would never do to confess that I could not find my way alone to the shanty, when I was so near to it. To my inexpressible relief, however, who should I find comfortably chatting and smoking with the master of the house but my good old friend, John Mc———, one of the teamsters in the very shanty to which I was going. I knew I was all right now. John, after an experience of thirty years shantying in this country, could go blindfold through its most intricate windings. My anxieties and fears vanished at once. What contemptible hypocrites we can become upon occasion. With an air of complete assurance and self-confidence, I saluted them, and said "I had just come in for a smoke and chat before going home."

As John and I tramped along through the deep gloaming, the hour and surroundings made us feel reflective and serious, and our conversation soon assumed the same character. It is astonishing too, how confidential and communicative you grow with a person when sitting or walking with him in the darkness.

John is a religious man in the true sense of the term. He is an honest, God-fearing, and simple-minded believer, and withal, a most tender and warm-hearted man. He is the worthy son of a most worthy sire, and of a mother whose name is a household word in all this community. There is no woman who has ever lived in Dalhousie who was more widely known, and highly esteemed and loved, and who is more missed, than kind, genial, motherly old Mrs.

Mc———. She was a favorite with every one, and every one seemed to be a favorite with her. She was as impartial as she was lavish in her kindly ministrations to every one who visited her place. No teamster need ever leave her house without a change of dry socks for his feet, and the loan of a warm muffler for his throat if the night was cold and damp. And yet she was so judicious in her attentions that each one thought he was the special object of her kindness. I labored under this delusion for many a year, until, when boasting about it to some of my friends, I found that each one of them entertained the same opinion about himself. And yet when we came to compare notes on the subject we found that the old lady had a good word for every one of us to the others. So we very logically came to the conclusion that there was no "blarney" about her, but her unvarying kindness to us was the outcome, pure and simple, of a warm, loving, and affectionate heart,—and such I honestly believe hers was.

As we tramped along John commenced to talk about his mother, a subject of which I, in common with many others, never tired of hearing. He gave me an account of her deathbed.

After a long and trying sickness, which she bore

with great patience and Christian cheerfulness, her end was visibly come. As John sat by her bedside holding her hand he asked her:

"Mother, do you know me?"

"Ah, John," she replied, "I ken you weel, I ken you all. But it is all darkness about me, and I am entering on that long, dark journey from which I can never come to you again."

"These were her last words," said John.

And, as he spoke, I knew by his voice that the tears were rolling down his bronzed cheeks.

Never was a mother held in more reverent and affectionate remembrance by her children, than she.

After a pause John resumed the conversation by somewhat abruptly saying: "The happiest and calmest deathbed I ever saw was that of my brother in-law, Jas. W——."

W—— was a man who was held in great esteem by his neighbors for his honest, straightforward, and consistent demeanor. He was a faithful husband and father, a kindly neighbor, and a warm, zealous member of the church. For two years he had been battling with the fell scourge, consumption, but the disease had become too deeply seated in his system, and though only a little over the prime of life, it was too evident that his days, nay, his hours, were numbered.

On the morning of the day of his death, John, who had been unremitting in his attendance upon him, paid him his customary daily visit. He found him much worse, in truth in great suffering, and evidently near his end.

In answer to John's question whether he had settled all his affairs, he replied he had not, and requested that they might at once be attended to. After this business was fully and satisfactorily attended to in the presence of all his family, who stood weeping round his bed, he said, "John, I must now compose my mind for death and eternity."

"Are you suffering much pain, James?" John asked him.

"Yes," was the reply, "but nothing to what my Saviour suffered for me."

Then, turning his face to the wall, he lay for a long time, apparently in deep meditation. All at once, in a clear, sweet tone he exclaimed:

"Do you see yon bright star, John?"

"No, James, I cannot see it."

"Ah John, that's my home, my home, my home;" and with the words he breathed his last.

When John gently turned him over, his spirit indeed had flown to its bright starry home above.

" Those were his last words," said John, "and they have been sounding in my ears ever since."

And so they have in mine, too, as uttered in the darkling night, in the deep, homely, reverent tone of John's Scottish accent.

Reader, when you and I come to die may we, with as much simple faith and assurance, and with our eye fixed on some bright star above, be enabled to say, " that's my home, my home, my home."

CHAPTER VII.

Old Saint-Saint, the Hermit.

ONE of the peculiarities of a shanty establishment is the old supernumerary that is often attached to it.

Almost every long-established concern has some old faithful servant, incapacitated from active work and grown grey in the service, who still remains connected with it as a kind of pensioner upon its bounty. He has been so long in the harness, his habits have so moulded and ironed him, that he must die where he has lived. At the solicitation of friends or relatives he goes to the settlements, and thinks he will end his days amid its comfortable environments, but he finds it an impossibility. Its restraints and proprieties are irksome to him; he "doesn't understand," and "doesn't like the ways of the town's-folk." His heart is in the woods. His speech, manners, thoughts, associations, habits, and enjoyments are all there. He would rather have cold pork and beans, than roast beef and turkey. His hard bunk in shanty or hut is sweeter to him, than the down and feathers of the sweetest and cosiest bedroom. He seems to be dead to all ties of family and kinship, but keenly alive to those of nature and the wild woods.

And here a noticeable feature of the shantyman's character is observable : no matter how gruff and unsociable, and even morose, the old man may be— and he is sometimes extremely so—he is always treated with kindness and consideration and, sometimes, as in the case of my old friend Date, with great respect, and his opinion often requested, and deferred to.

It must not be supposed, however, that these old gentlemen are useless appendages to the establishment. By no means ; in some instances the old supernumerary is the most useful man about the place. He generally makes his habitat about the farm or depot of the concern ; and though he receives no pay, nor indeed wants any, yet he repays his board and clothing many times over by looking after the cattle and poultry, and attending to the thousand odds and ends of little work, which necessarily belong to such an establishment,—and this, too, with a judgment and economy which a younger and less experienced man could not practise. In these departments, also, he is often very despotic and touchy as to his authority.

I remember well how old Date would brook no interference, or meddling in the farm-yard at the Black River depot. The calves and poultry were the special objects of his care, and if Jim and I wanted some variety in our menu we had always to ask Date's permission before we could lay murderous hands upon calf or chicken. It was most amusing to hear him abusing and swearing at John, the foreman of the farm, and ordering him off about his business if he happened to come about when he was busy with his charges, which, to John's credit be it said, he always took with good-humor and playful repartee.

One of the best specimens of this class is old Saint-Saint the Hermit. Saint-Saint, however, is a retired old gentleman of independent home and position. Though he has been engaged during the active part of his life in shanty business, yet he preferred, when the infirmities of old age came upon him, to retire altogether from its active scenes, and live apart and alone, in a hut of his own construction, in an isolated and retired locality.

His hut, about ten feet square, and snug and comfortable enough, stands in rather a romantic position two miles below Joe's lake, about the middle of what is called the Long Stretch, which is an

Old Saint Saint, the Hermit.

expansion of the Clide between two rapids some three miles apart.

The accompanying picture, taken from life, gives an admirable likeness of the Hermit's face, and when you add to this a lithe, active, medium-sized frame, without any apparent symptoms of imbecility either of mind or body, you have old Saint-Saint. And yet he is over eighty years of age, and for twenty years has led the life of a recluse in this locality.

His history is one of the most singularly unromantic you ever heard in your life. He has a wife and large family living on a comfortable farm near Montreal. The former he has not seen for twenty-five years, and the reason he left her was not because she was unfaithful, or extravagant, or unkind, or any other of the common-place frailties of womankind, but because she was too saving of his hard-earned wages. When he would give her money on his return from the shanty, or send it to her, she was in the habit of putting it out at interest, on good security, without telling him anything about it. Whatever was her motive in this, it was, as far as I could learn, the only ground of disturbance between them,—otherwise she was, even according to Saint-Saint's account, an exemplary wife and mother in all respects. He is, however, very reticent about this, and all other personal matters.

Be the cause what it may, the old fellow left wife, and children, and home, and, burying himself in this isolated retreat, refused to have any further intercourse with them. His wife has made repeated overtures for reconciliation, but in vain; and though one of his sons came to see him a few years ago, and brought clothes and money, yet he told him never to come back, and not to "bother" him any more. He lays no claim to his property, but allows his wife and children to do as they please with it. Altogether his mode of existence is a strange freak of human nature, and quite unaccountable on any of the grounds from which people generally take enjoyment and satisfaction out of life; but that is his business, and, if he likes it better than any other, let him by all means enjoy it.

There is nothing morose, or melancholy, or even unsocial about the old fellow, and whatever feeling of pity you may have for him in the abstract is quickly dispelled when you visit him. He is a lively, merry, crickety old fellow, full of hospitality, chatty and glad to see you. He is, withal, a vanity-stricken old man, as was plainly shewn by the readiness with which he acceded to the artist's proposal to draw his portrait, and the patience and grave complacency with which he sat for hours while the picture was being executed. The artist very kindly promised to send him a copy afterwards, and this gave him unbounded satisfaction.

He supports himself by hunting, trapping and fishing, but mainly the latter, as his eyesight and nerve are failing him, so that he has great difficulty in handling the rifle or gun. I always take him some tea and pork when I go to see him, which he most gratefully receives, as also the contributions which his kindly French neighbours give him.

On the occasion of my last visit to him, I was, and had been for weeks, suffering from a severe cold and cough. With the respect which we instinctively pay to an octogenarian, and a hermit, I asked him for a remedy, which he at once gave, with a simplicity and gravity which commanded esteem and confidence. It was this:—" Take five drinks of cold water every morning before breakfast for nine consecutive days." I did so—at least I drank as much cold water as I could comfortably contain— and as sure as anything under the sun I got entirely rid of my cold before the nine days were up, and I havn't had a bark, or a symptom of it, since. I intend to get some more remedies from the old

Hermit before I leave, and if they only prove as efficacious as this one, I may safely take Asclepiades, wager against Fortune, that "I will never be ill as long as I live."

With all the bodily comfort they can possibly secure, and all the contentment and ease of life which they can reasonably expect, still the condition of these old recluses of the forest is one of peculiarly melancholy and lonesome interest. I have stood by their graves—the graves of some whom I have known long and loved well—and among the saddest thoughts I ever had I felt, as I stood there. In the still solemn depths of the forest, far removed from human ken and life, in sight of the crumbling ruins of the old hut in which they lived and died—by the lonely side of some rock-bound lake over which they had fished and shot—on some jutting headlands of the Madawaska and Matawan, from which you can look for leagues over a mighty landscape of forest, water and mountain, and detect no sign of man's presence or work, those graves are found—uncared-for, unknown, forgotten, fitting memorials of the lonesome, forsaken life the old man lived and loved.

It's all very well as long as these old men enjoy a fair measure of health and substantial vigor—then we can understand how, to a person of a certain constitution, there would be some satisfaction, and even positive enjoyment, in the life; but when sickness comes, as come it does upon occasion, even to the most healthy and robust,—when failing senses and abatement of strength set in,—then they must have many wearisome seasons of despondency and apprehensive reflection, and an intense longing for the company, sympathy, and help of their kindred and fellow-creatures. Their daily life, too, is one of continual danger to life or limb: the fall of a tree or branch, a sudden squall on the lake, the bursting of a gun, a tumble off a high log, and a dozen other casualties incident to backwoods life, may kill in a moment or so maim them that they may be laid up for weeks or months, and during this time not a living soul may come near them or know anything about their condition,—in such straights as these they must feel lonely and wretched to the last degree.

Take it all in all, their life is more to be pitied than envied, and more to be reprehended than respected. But who knows the deep workings, the self-impelling motives, the sensitive shrinkings, and, maybe, the unhealed scars of the human heart! These old recluses have a reason for their lives that is, at all events, satisfactory to themselves, and, if we can't understand or commend it, let us at least keep one's own counsel, and extend to them all tender sympathy, all kindly cheer, and all the practical help that their age and loneliness demand; and the good Lord who knows all secrets, and tenderly loves all His creatures, will not overlook nor forget.

CHAPTER VIII.

Forest Fires.

IT would be a very easy matter to go into rhapsodies over the sublime spectacle of a fire in the forest. This, however, has been done so often and in so much better style than I can possibly emulate, and withal it can be so readily taken in by an ordinary imagination that comprehends the terrible nature and effects of fire when it has illimitable inflammable material to feed upon, that it is needless for me to attempt to depict it. Anyway, I am so greatly impressed with the terribly stern, practical nature of this question, and of its urgent claims upon the attention of all thinking Canadians, that I feel I have no time in dealing with it for mere figures of speech and pretty descriptions. I have seen a mighty forest bathed in a sea of angry fire, and, with all its grand, unutterable sublimity, I never wish to see it again.

Forest fires have been, and are still, a crying disgrace to the government and people of Canada. It is almost incredible to think that people's eyes and minds have never been fairly opened to the extent and magnitude of this terrible evil, which has devastated such a vast extent of our most valuable territory, and robbed us of untold millions of hard cash.

In order to present this subject in its clearest light we shall look at in a three-fold point of view, viz.: first, the origin of forest fires; second, the destructive extent of them; and, third, the approximate preventive of them.

First, as to the origin of forest fires, many, and some very plausible, theories are expressed, such as ignition of the trees during a thunder-storm by the lightning, camp and mid-day fires by hunters, bush-rangers and Indians, and neglected fires of any kind by stray tramps or others through the forest. Now there is no doubt that any one of these causes may, upon occasion, have been sufficient of itself to have started a fire, and a most destructive one too, but, take them one and all, I regard those primal agents of the evil as mere casualties, as accidental things, which are beyond the scope of legislation and human prevention, and which have occurred, and, do what we may, always will occur while the forest stands; but I am very far from attaching the importance to them which some do, as being the main factors in causing these fearful conflagrations which have ravaged our most valuable pineries and other woods.

I believe that not only are they of rare occurrence, but that the destructive extent of the fires caused by these agents can be narrowed down to a comparatively small, perhaps insignificant, area.

The real origin of our appalling forest fires is traceable, directly or indirectly, to the *settlers of the country*, either in their spring or summer fallows in clearing the land, or, occasionally, in making potash. One presumptive proof of the correctness of this theory is the undeniable fact that in those sections of Canada where the settler has not yet penetrated and located, there have been no great general conflagrations. The forest, in these sections, at least as compared with those in the settled districts, are in their virgin condition of greenness, and in this condition they remain until we hear of settlers moving in, and then we too often hear, at no very distant date subsequently, the wretched tale of fire and devastation.

And when we look at this matter of the settler from another point of view, viz., their rank, inexcusable, criminal carelessness in starting and attending to their fires, the wonder is that the destruction caused by them is not infinitely greater than what it actually is. I have been amazed beyond measure at the wanton, thoughtless, perverse folly—you may call it stupid madness, no term is too strong for it—

of some of our backwoods settlers in handling and "putting out" fire in the woods around them. There is a terrible selfishness in it, too, which makes it thoroughly criminal. The only precaution that these people adopt is to see that their own buildings and belongings are safe ; as long as the fire keeps away from them they don't seem to care where it goes, how far it spreads, who it damages, or what destruction it causes.

A settler cuts down and makes ready for burning a block, we will say, of ten acres or more of his land ; at the first favorable opportunity or wind, that is, for his own convenience and safety, he "puts out," as they say, though it is a frightful misnomer, the fire, quite regardless of its close proximity to, sometimes touching in fact, the most extensive, inflammable and valuable forests. They will even assist at times the natural tendency of the fire to go in this direction ; for, instead of cutting the trees so as to fall within the circle of their clearing, they will often allow them to fall with their top branches into the woods beyond, and even throw out upon them the loose, dry, dead limbs that may be in their way. I have seen a deep, high, brush wall of the most ignitable material all round the borders of such a clearance, and only wanting the smallest spark to set it ablaze, and spread far and wide a terrible conflagration. A very little attention and additional labor on the part of the settler would at times prevent a destruction of timber property which may be reckoned by tens of thousands of dollars, yes, and sometimes infinitely more.

This leads us to my *second point* of observation on this question, viz.: the *destructive extent* of our forest fires.

It is simply appalling to take a bird's-eye view of a tract of country that has been devastated by the fire fiend. From an æsthetic standpoint it is dreary, desolate, uninviting, even repelling in the highest degree; but to look at it in a matter of fact, economical, and sound business manner, it is disheartening, nay, maddening in the extreme.

You take your stand on the peak of some lofty hill from which you can take in the country in every direction for miles around: nothing is to be seen but dead, burnt, black pineries and other precious woods. Some are still standing, altogether or partially denuded of their limbs — "rampikes" we call them — and the country before us is a "brule;" others, and vast quantities, are lying on the ground, where we see in pitiful advantage their huge, gigantic proportions. The ground is so thickly covered that we can walk along them in a zig-zag direction for a mile at a stretch without touching the earth. Between the standing and lying timber we see at one glance a sum in loss and loss which our utmost calculating ability cannot solve.

Let me try to give some approximate estimate of the loss that has been incurred. Remember, we are taking a fair average pine country, and one, also, from which so little timber has been utilized that the amount is only a fraction compared to what has been burnt.

It is generally estimated that each acre of such a country will yield six sound trees of white or red pine, that is, 600 trees for a lot of 100 acres. Now, when one lumber merchant sues another for trespass on his limits—which is quite a common transaction—and obtains judgment against him, he is allowed by law $4 a stump for the damage done. At this figure a pine lot of 100 acres would be worth $2,400, and a square mile, that is 640 acres, $15,360. Now how many square miles do you take in from your point of view on the eminence we spoke of—say it is only ten,—here then you take at one glance a destruction caused by fire of upwards of $150,000.

Extending our range of mental observation and calculation, how many square miles of burnt pine lands are there in the Ottawa Valley? Put it at the moderate figure of 4000, and we find that the bulk total of the damage done by this foul scourge swells up to the enormous sum of over $60,000,000. This, however, is not a fair way of getting at the true estimate of the money loss to the country through fire. Take sixty-five feet as the average per stick of all the timber that has been taken out of the Ottawa Valley for the last twenty-five years, and 15 cts. per foot as the average price got in Quebec, and calculating sawn lumber at very much the same aggregate value, this gives $10 as the value of a sound pine tree, instead of $4. This calculation at once swells the aggregate loss by fire to over $150,000,000, or six times as much as the Government's cash grant to build the Canada Pacific Railway.

And yet these gigantic figures, representing a national and commercial value which the mind cannot grasp, especially in a young and struggling country like Canada, are referable only to the Ottawa Valley, and take no cognizance of the losses by fire in many parts of Quebec, and the northwestern part of Ontario.

I do not wish to stun and weary the reader with ponderous numerical magnitudes, and enough has been said to show the incalculable and heartsickening loss and destruction caused by our forest fires. Let us come then to the third, and most important, point, viz.: the *approximate preventive* of these fires. I use the word approximate advisedly, for no matter what precautions we adopt we never will be able to prevent the periodical recurrence of fires in the woods of a greater or less magnitude.

As I ascribe the main cause of these fires to the settler, so it is with him that we mainly have to deal in any precautionary and preventive measures that should be adopted. If the settler could only be induced to give some care and labor to the *preparing of his clearance for fires*, after the trees are cut down and piled up, the risk of fire spreading from it would be very largely, if not altogether, diminished. I have already hinted at this, but it cannot be too repeatedly and strongly urged upon him.

To have his fallow complete, and safe for burning, he should have every tree on its margin so cut as to fall inwards and not outwards, and all the underbrush and loose branches thrown well into the heap. This being done, he should dig and turn up the moist earth in a complete circle round the clearing,—this operation, which would not cost more than two days' work for two men, would keep the fire within certain bounds, and almost ensure, in favorable weather, against the risk of spreading.

But as selfishness and cupidity are the strongest incentives to action where the interests of the whole are concerned—and nowhere does this principle operate more strongly than among our backwoods settlers—we would advocate the giving of *all the dues* collected by the Government on the timber cut on the settler's land to the settler himself, or placed to his credit for the payment of his land. This naturally would have the effect of causing the settler to entertain a good feeling towards both the Government and the lumber merchant, and making him exceedingly careful in protecting the timber on his land, and, consequently, that on every side of him. Again when we look at this proposition in a kindly, economic point of view, what a mighty boon would this grant (say if only forty dollars a year) be to the poor struggling settler? Why it would keep his family in flour and tea for the whole year, or buy him a yoke of steers to do his "logging" for him; and, on the other hand, taking the aggregate of all the dues collected from all the settlers in the Ottawa Valley by the Government for one year, what a comparatively insignificant sum would it be out of the Treasury chest. In 1881 the sum thus collected amounted to less than $10,000, what a paltry amount is this, in view of even the *probable* prevention of fires in the forest, any one of which might cause the lumber merchant, and through him the country at large, the loss of double that amount; and what a relief and practical assistance to the settlers would this sum be when parceled out to each in the probable proportion we mentioned. We are aware that some persons argue that giving these dues to the settlers would have the very opposite effect from that which we are predicating. That it would induce many of them purposely to "put out" fire in order to burn the pine, so that the lumber merchants would be compelled, in their own interests, to send in a large force of men the first season after, in order to cut it down and secure it before it would be destroyed by the worm, which it generally is, if left standing for two seasons after the fire has taken place, and thus the settler would at once pocket (if the dues went to him) a handsome sum. But though isolated cases of this kind may have occurred, still we have a better opinion of the average settler than to believe this dastardly, unprincipled thing of him. And anyway he has sense enough to see what a short-sighted, penny-wise-pound-foolish policy this would be. In all probability he would lose some valuable portion of his pine and other woods, even with the utmost exertions of the merchant to utilise them; and, besides, he could calculate with *no certainty* upon the merchant *cutting a single tree* of his burnt woods—the latter's arrangements for the season, and a hundred other causes, might prevent him doing this; in this case the damage, both directly and indirectly, would fall back upon himself.

But, after all that can be said and done, I hold that the *surest preventive* of forest fires of any great extent is, the *judicious and adequate appointment* of fire inspectors. In this matter the Government have been exceedingly blameworthy, or have acted with a terribly ignorant, blind-fold sort of policy. The laws they have enacted on the question are a farce and a failure, for the simple reason that they never have, nor never can, be enforced under the present system. No settler will ever inform on his neighbor, no matter what reward is offered, and even the lumber merchant, whose limits have been ravaged from end to end, will take no active measures to bring the culprit to justice, even though he knows who he is. And those who understand the nature of the question, and all its bearings and surroundings in the backwoods, cannot blame these parties either for their inaction in the matter. I believe that not a *single fire has ever been prevented*, or a *single dollar's worth of timber saved to the country by all the laws the Government have ever passed, or by all* **the** *inspection they have ever* **appointed.**

If the Government are really in earnest in this matter, what they ought to do is to appoint a *considerable number* of inspectors, and allocate to each **one a** special section of country over which he is to exercise supervision and jurisdiction. These sections should not be of too extended an area, but of such an extent as, in the judgment of competent **persons, could** easily be supervised by one inspector. Take, for instance, the country lying between the Mississippi and the Madawaska, which **has been**, and is to a large extent still, the most valuable timber region of all Canada, and which also **has** been and is still, almost yearly, the **arena of fearful** conflagrations: how many inspectors would it require to keep a watchful eye over this section during the dangerous **fire** seasons of the year, viz., about six weeks in early **spring, and** two months in mid-summer; for these two periods **cover the** ground during which almost every fire breaks out. I would say that ten men who thoroughly understood their business would be amply sufficient. Su**p**pose you pay these men $200 each for his three or four months' service, that is $2,000 yearly; **what** a mere bagatelle is this compared with the security and incalculable money profit that would accrue to the country. Adopting the same principle of action for the whole Ottawa valley —suppose this general inspection would cost $20,000 (which we think would cover the amount), how easily this could be balanced in the treasury accounts by the smallest additional fraction upon the timber dues.

The Government spare no expense in sending out cullers and other officials in order to secure their revenue from the lumber merchants, and yet, with regard to the great essential point, yea the very vitality of the revenue, they exhibit the most negligent and inexcusable remissness. We talk about the penny-wise-and-pound-foolish conduct of the settlers, why, it is reduced to the minimum, compared to the maximum of folly, which the Government are guilty of in this question.

As to the personnel of these inspectors, the Government should exercise the utmost discretion and impartial discrimination. It won't do to send out men from Toronto, or, in fact, from any towns or cities, or mere lackies or Government hangers-on. We don't want men who will come out with gun, fishing-tackle, tent and servant, merely to have a good time in the woods. No, these inspectors should be appointed from the *backwoods*, men who are experienced bush-rangers of practical knowledge and judgment, who understand all about the "putting out" of fire, as well as the checking and extinguishing of it, whether large or small. Men who, with their axe on their shoulder and pack on their back, will range continually through their allotted section, and sleep out, if need be, every night of the fire season. There are plenty of such men to be found in the lumbering country, especially at these seasons, when the winter's work is over. I would have no difficulty in laying my hands upon twenty such men at a week's notice, who would gladly undertake the work and responsibility for the remuneration I spoke of.

As I intimated, the duties of these men should include jurisdiction, that is, they should have the authority of arresting and prosecuting any settler or others whom they should find infringing the fire laws. They should be held responsible for any fire that breaks out, as far as discovering the originator is concerned, and, if there is any culpability in the matter, of bringing him to justice. One or two stringent examples, say of penitentiary for two years, would have a mighty influence in bringing careless and criminal parties to their proper senses as to the way in which they should handle fire in the woods. And if it were thoroughly understood that these inspectors had this power, and were obligated by oath of office to exercise it, then no offence could be taken, no odium incurred, but, on the contrary, they would gain the esteem and approval of all right-thinking persons in the community. The moment an inspector discovers a fire in his section—which he can easily do in this country of hills and mountains, by the smoke—he should hasten to the spot, and, if it is an ordinary settler's fire for clearing, see that all lawful precautions are being adopted, and if it is likely to extend, and he finds it is impossible for him to manage it single-handed, then he should have the authority of engaging men at a fixed rate to assist him. Half-a-dozen men, rightly directed, can check almost any fire if taken in reasonable time.

Another duty of these inspectors should be to prevent settlers from securing patents for lots which are pure and simple timber lands. I hold strong views on this point of the question. If, twenty-five years ago, the Government had enacted that the greater portion of the Ottawa Valley should be held as a timber reserve, and nothing else—in other words, allowed no settlers in it, it would have been one of the wisest, most far-seeing, and beneficent enactments ever passed by any Government—the wisest and the best for the settlers themselves, the Government, and the country generally. The Ottawa Valley was **never** intended to be, and all the industry and capital in the world never will make it be, an agricultural country; but if **it** had been reserved **for** the utilizing of its natural capabilities and resources, viz., lumber of every description, what an incalculable mine of wealth **would it have been** to-day for the Dominion. This is at once obvious, even to the most superficial reflector and calculator. But it is **not** too late to enact some such proviso still. There **are** hundreds of Government lots yet in the market **that are** utterly worthless, except for the lumber **that is on them,** but are immensely **valuable in** this respect. Now no settlement in the way **of** clearing land for agricultural purposes should be allowed **on** these lots. Such **a** proviso would not only minimise the risk from **fire, but it would also** prevent the settlers from selfishly and criminally speculating on **the** timber, merely for the sake of the Government dues, **which on** such lots would amount to a very large **sum.** I could point out on the map certain lots of a hundred acres where the lumber merchant has taken off timber which has yielded dues to the amount of over $2,000, and these are not rare or exceptional cases. Now the Government would have **a** perfect right to protect itself, and the country, from unprincipled speculations on the part of the settlers in this point of view, and it could easily do this by ordering the inspectors to prevent settlement on these lots. This would be no injustice to any intending settler; if he wishes a homestead for a farm, then the Government will give him every facility for gratifying his desire in the most rich and eligible location. And if he is an honest man, and wishes to make money out of the lumber business proper, then let him go to the merchant on whose limits such a lot as we speak of may be, and make an open bargain with him, either for a job, or to buy a "cut," or purchase out and out the whole lot for a stated sum; but don't let him attempt to cheat both the Government and the merchant by pretending to take out the lot for farming purposes, while all the time he is looking after only the dues on the timber, and thus, in every probability, inflicting an immense loss upon both parties, merely for the sake of pocketing himself a few hundred dollars. Now, it would be an easy matter, as we have said, for the fire inspector to have his eye on these lots, and see that no settlement takes place on them, either by squatter or Government patentee, but that they are reserved and utilized according to their natural and legitimate purpose.

I conclude my views on this subject by emphasizing in the strongest possible manner the great necessity that exists *at this present time* for the enactment of the most stringent and imperative laws and precautions with respect to forest fires. Never, since the lumbering business commenced in the Ottawa Valley, has the country, particularly to the south of the river, been more ripe and ready for terrible conflagrations than at the present moment. Fearful as these have been in the past, they are nothing compared to what may break out at any hour, and at innumerable places, in the immediate future. These great fires have piled up on the land immense masses of the most inflammable material, which need only a spark to set them into a blaze. The fire has only half done its work; it has singed, but not cindered, vast pineries and swamps; it has charred, but not reduced to ashes, vast tracts of forest; it has left in its wake a region that is so dry, and dead, and inflammable that I have often wondered why, in the hot scorching weeks of midsummer, it did not burst into flames by spontaneous ignition. Under certain conditions of accident, of weather, of settlement, of carelessness, we may yet witness, and that before long, the most appalling and wide-spread conflagration that has ever yet devastated the **Ottawa Valley.** All these contingencies are intensified by the fact of the Kingston and Pembroke Railway now running through the very heart of this highly inflammable region. Hence I maintain that, if ever the Government were called upon to adopt and enforce the most stringent precautionary measures with respect to fires in the woods, it is at this present time.

Again, how much is this obligation heightened by the consideration—not generally understood or known—of the immense quantities of most valuable timber that still remains in this country? From the account I have given of the destructive extent of forest fires, the reader may be disposed to think that there cannot be much timber left in the country to be burnt; but, notwithstanding all the fearful conflagrations that have swept over the land, and the incalculable damage done, still it is amazing the vast quantities of pine and other woods that yet remain. Every one who is acquainted with the lumbering country knows well how often the cry is raised, "the timber supply of this country is exhausted, we must go further and far back to get enough of pine to make the business pay." I have heard this old story repeated regularly, season after season, for the last twenty years; and yet the fact is that many limits which have been "culled" over and over again, and abandoned as worthless, or sold at small figures, are being to-day most profitably worked, and yielding every year large rafts of square timber and hundreds of thousands of logs. No doubt the average of size and finenesss of quality are greatly deteriorated, but neither the producer nor the buyer are so particular now as they used to be. If they cannot get exactly what they would like, they just have to like what they can get; and the truth is that, after all the burning, and culling, and supposed exhaustion, what they do get is not such a bad article after all, and, as I have said, is in good paying quantities, too.

There is, besides, another element of supply which now, and only very lately, is entering largely into the calculations of the lumber merchant, and that is the *utilizing of the lying timber*, for saw-logs especially. It is now ascertained that vast quantities of fallen pine, which had been abandoned years ago as utterly worthless, contain some of the best and soundest lumber. I have seen, during this season, on the Caldwell limits, immense trunks of trees that were cut or blown down forty years ago, being sawn into logs, and found to be among the best that can be cut. This is particularly the case with trees that are lying in low moist ground. An inch or two on the surface are indeed rotten, but the sap seems to have collected and hardened there, and formed a kind of cement, which has preserved the heart and great bulk of the tree sound, and free from worms. From this point of view, there is no calculation where and when the lumber supply may cease, for the quantity of fallen trees, good, bad, and inferior, is absolutely incalculable.

Now, if such a conflagration as we speak of and dread should break out, this fallen timber would have to bear its full share of destruction; and, between standing and lying timber, the absolute money loss to the country would be fearful beyond all calculation.

CHAPTER IX.

A Sunday Service in the Shanty.

AS may be very readily understood, it is a very difficult thing, and, in certain seasons of the year, quite impossible, to maintain regular stated services in these backwoods. And, as for the shanties, services are never held, except on casual occasions by individuals, and only at great intervals, or by the instrumentality of the Lumberman's Mission, which is an attempt by the Presbyterian Church to overtake this wide and scattered field.

Whenever, and wherever, I found it expedient and agreeable to the men, I have held services, esteeming it both a privilege and a duty to do so.

You require to exercise a good deal of judgment, both as to the time and manner of conducting these services. They must be short, interesting and to the point, and at such an hour as will not interfere with the men's ordinary Sunday avocations, at least such as are necessary and, under the circumstances, innocent, such as washing their clothes, going to the post office, writing their letters and visiting friends and relations in the surrounding shanties, or among the settlers in the neighborhood. I found that ten o'clock in the morning was always the best hour to suit all parties. It allowed the men time for a prolonged and comfortable sleep, and left the afternoon free for their accustomed avocations, and socialities.

Some of the most enjoyable services I ever held have been on these occasions. One in particular I shall never forget. It was on the first Sunday after my arrival at Manahan's shanty. Full notice had been given, and over one hundred men assembled from the different shanties, and railroad works in the vicinity.

A more respectful, attentive, and apparently devout audience I never preached to. There was not the least levity, nor anything approaching the unbecoming from beginning to end. Tom, the blacksmith from the mill works, acted as precentor, and with a voice and a style that would have done credit to any city professional. As the strong, bass voices joined in with his deep mellow tones in Old Hundred, the grand old melody rolled forth into the surrounding forest with sublime and touching effect.

My subject was the longevity of the antediluvian forefathers, and the contrast between it and our present comparatively short-lived existence. The subject is naturally full of many interesting phases

of human life, and replete with wholesome lessons
on its shortness and uncertainty, and thus, in many
points, was specially applicable to the dangerous and
adventurous lives of most of my hearers. If close
and earnest attention is any gratification to a preacher
—and what preacher living is not gratified with it—
I certainly had it; and also the comments, which I
casually overheard after service, and which were as
genuine as they were characteristic, were not un-
gratifying if they were *peculiar:* " faith he's a roarer
at the preachin'," "didn't he pave it down lively?"
" he knows how to put the fright on a fellow," &c., &c.

As I have said, the direct, conversational and
familiar style of preaching is the best adapted to
secure the attention and interest of these men. In
this they greatly resemble the soldiers, and I found
that my nine years' experience of preaching to the
latter was greatly to my advantage in addressing
them. There is such a thing, however, as carrying
this style of preaching to an extreme that is neither
edifying nor in good taste, as I one day had the
opportunity of hearing.

Some years ago, when I was on one of my fall
backwoods' excursions, I happened to be camped
over Sunday on *Caliboggie* Lake. Hearing that there
was to be "preachin'" at a school-house about a

mile away I started off to attend it. I found about a dozen people assembled, and after a few minutes the minister arrived.

He was quite a young man, just fresh from college, if indeed he had ever been in such an institution, and was a capital type of that pioneer class of preachers that you sometimes meet with in the far backwoods, and there only. He was lean, fiery-eyed, and full of zeal. He had preached already that day, had ridden over twenty miles, and had an appointment again for the evening. His whole appearance impressed you with the idea that he was a man whose whole soul was in his work, that he was untiring in the performance of it, and that he would even love to be a martyr in its hardships. I shall never forget his sermon. It was a strange compound of illogical, disconnected, incongruous odds and ends; and yet it was brimful of a kind of rough eloquence, of fanciful conceits, of impassioned fervor, and direct personalities. In illustrating the love of God he said, looking at the same time directly at a rather well-proportioned, good-looking young man, who was evidently wrapped up in the sermon, "God, instead of making you what you are, tall, stately and handsome, might have done the very reverse, he might have formed you crippled and hideous, in fact as ugly as *Old Nick*."

Suddenly turning from this subject, he launched off into another, which had no possible connection with it, viz.: the illuminating power of the Holy Spirit. From the look in his eye, and general tone, I suspected he was about to favor us with another personality, and so he did with a *vim* and a directness that struck home with a vengeance.

About the middle of the building, which was not more than fourteen feet by twelve, a tall shantyman was seated on one of the benches, with his back against the writing-desk, and his long legs stretched out halfway across the floor. The man was paying little attention to the sermon, but was most industriously chewing tobacco, and squirting the juice with great force and precision at some imaginary object between his outspread toes. I saw that the minister's wrath was kindling against him, and that he was revolving in his mind how he could fire a shot at him. At this juncture the sermon took the turn I have indicated, and our zealous exhorter delivered his fire in certainly a most striking and practical manner. "There was a certain godly minister," he said, "who was so illuminated by the Holy Spirit that he knew for certain that a particular individual in the congregation was chewing tobacco and spitting the vile stuff all over the floor," looking as he spoke directly in the face of the offending party. The effect upon the latter was electrical. With a muttered oath he drew up his long legs with a sudden jerk, and reddened with confusion and anger. And the minister, apparently re-invigorated by the startling effect of his rebuke, proceeded on in his erratic, impassioned course.

It jarred, however, upon my ears, and, I have no doubt, upon those of the rest of the audience, and spoiled the effect of what, in some respects, was otherwise a useful and practical sermon.

It would ill become me, however, to speak in the slightest disparaging terms of the general labors and effects of these backwoods preachers. They do a work amid discouragement, and toil, and absolute privation, which many of their brethren have neither the courage to attempt, nor the hardihood and patience to endure.

They are the "fags" of the Church, ill-paid, often ill-received, poorly-lodged, weather-beaten and travel worn; yet they toil on unremittingly and uncomplainingly, and do really a glorious work. They keep alive the knowledge of the Gospel and the light of salvation, in the dreary wastes of those outskirts of the land, and cheer and instruct many a lonely and darkened soul.

CHAPTER X.

Gentlemen Settlers.

ONE of the peculiar features of the backwoods country in the Ottawa Valley, is the number of old deserted clearings that you stumble upon in your wanderings through the bush. You light upon them often in the most unexpected and chance manner. Travelling leisurely and aimlessly through the deep, dense forest you emerge suddenly upon an open cleared space, far removed from any house or public highway. You wonder where you have come to now; you look about for signs of life and human presence, but all is still and silent as a churchyard. A strange eerie feeling of loneliness comes over you. What does it all mean?

The clearing may be a very large one, embracing perhaps a hundred acres, or it may contain only twenty or thirty, but, large or small, you soon discern unmistakable evidences of past human settlement and activity.

The gigantic pine and hemlock have all been cut down and cleared away. The margin of the native forest is as sharply and clearly defined as if it had been mown down by the scythe of some mighty Titan. A dense scrubby undergrowth of pine, balsam, spruce, in fact of every tree of the surrounding bush, has grown up over the place. But here and there some grassy spots, the last relics of human culture, are still stoutly holding their own against this encroaching invasion of the sturdy saplings. About the centre of the clearing stand the old crumbling ruins of a former human habitation. Nothing may be left but the chimney, which had been built of stronger and more firmly cemented material, and a heap of moss-covered stones and old rotten timbers. It wanted but this to complete the utter loneliness of the spot. It was indeed a scene of dreary, lifeless, forsaken desolation, over which the silence of the grave reigned.

This, gentle reader, was once the home, I dare not say happy home, of a gentleman settler. This spot, along with many others I could picture, all tell the same old sad story of blighted hopes, of laborious but ill-directed exertions, of crushing and starving poverty.

A number of years ago, the then Minister of Agriculture, actuated no doubt by the best motives, and by what he thought was accurate information on the subject, resolved to colonize the neglected wastes of the Ottawa valley, and, if possible, by a superior class of emigrants from the Old Country. Accordingly, he published pamphlets and statistics on the country of the most glowing nature. Statistics can be so cooked as to mean anything, and, with ordinarily credulous people, can be so twisted as powerfully to promote any hobby which a prominent and influential man may adopt and determine to prosecute.

The Ottawa valley was depicted as the new Land of Promise; and the cry was sent across the waters, "come over and take possession, and you will gain all that the heart of man can desire in the way of comfort, prosperity and affluence."

No expense was spared. Agents were sent to every part of the United Kingdom, charged with the most promising inducements to every class, but especially the middle and richer, to embark their fortunes in this *terra optissima*.

In consequence, great numbers came over, and, without even going to the expense and trouble of investigating the country beforehand, took out patents for the locations they selected from government maps and plans, and at once moved in with their families and possessions.

The lots on which they located were, for the most part, densely wooded with pine and hemlock, often most difficult of access, and frequently at quite a distance from even the most primitive human settlements. The cutting down and "logging"—the general clearing off—of these mighty patriarchs of the forest was, in itself, a herculean task; but the expense that it involved to this special class of settlers was, perhaps, quadruple what it would have been to any other. Their inexperience, their former style of living, their repugnance to put up with the inconveniences and privations necessarily incident to such a position, and, absurd though it may sound, their desire to keep up appearances and show that they had money, and were superior to the miserably poor class that surrounded them, all led them, at the outset particularly, into lavish outlays and perfectly unnecessary expenses, which made serious inroads upon their capital. Personally, with many of them, it was all spend and no work, injudicious and worthless overseeing, and careless, half-performed service.

No doubt they were often most unfairly and dishonestly treated by their neighbors, and those with whom they had to deal. They were accounted fair game to pluck by many of these people, and, in fact, a kind of God-send, in a money point of view, to a hard-working, poor and struggling community.

All this, however, they bore with true British pluck and even cheerfulness, buoyed up with the hope that, when the land was finally cleared, they would be in possession of a "fine estate" of two or three hundred acres, on which they would live in comfort and affluence, and hand down as a noble heritage to their children. But, as year after year rolled away, the conviction gradually dawned upon them that those hopes were never to be realized. The land was, doubtless, cleared, but it was *land*, not soil, only a crust with no substratum of richness and fertility.

There are some of the saddest histories in connection with experiences of this kind that have ever been written. Histories of long years of patient waiting, of hard toiling, of menial drudging, of privation, sickness and absolute want; and, after all was done and endured, to find that they might as well have thrown their money and labor into the Ottawa, as far as any substantial fruit or return was realized.

I have no hesitation in saying, because I am borne out by personal acquaintance, and by the authority of those who know this country intimately for the last forty years, that *not one-fourth of even the cleared land of the Ottawa valley is fit for cultiva-*

tion, and many put it at a much lower proportion. No doubt, for two or three years after it is cleared it may yield fairly good crops, but it is of too light a nature, and too shallow in depth, to guarantee continuance and permanency of production.

Some townships there are, doubtless, of very rich soil, and where the farmers are well off and are among the most intelligent and influential agricultural communities of the Dominion, as Bathurst, most of Ramsay, part of Beckwith and Horton, Westmeath, &c., but these are oases in the vast sterile wilderness both north and south of the Ottawa.

It is pitiful to think of the incalculable amount of capital of every kind, intelligence, labor and money, both public and private, that have been absolutely wasted in this region. No greater mistake was ever made in political economy than the attempt to open up and colonize this country with the view of developing its agricultural resources; and, not only so, but these attempts, practically abortive as they have proved, have been the direct cause of entailing the loss of millions of treasure to the country, as we shall presently see.

The Ottawa Valley is essentially a lumbering region, the most valuable, both as to extent and quality, which is in the world—that is, it was so, but, alas, it is so no longer. The fire fiend has devastated it from end to end, from centre to circumference. There has been more timber destroyed by this terrible scourge than has ever been cut by the axe of the lumberer. Now, if these colonization efforts for the purpose of developing the agricultural resources had been directed to the proper localities of our country, such as western Ontario, and many sections of Quebec, where the true land for settlement at that time, and even yet in many parts is to be found, it would have been infinitely better for the settlers themselves and the country at large. Not only were vast quantities of the most valuable timber wantonly destroyed in the direct process of clearing the land, but, both directly and indirectly, as we have already shown in a previous chapter, the settlers have been the means of starting those terrible conflagrations which have swept over vast tracts, and made bare and worthless thousands of square miles. It is absolutely impossible to estimate the actual money loss to the country which has been incurred through these fires, and which, I believe, would, in a large measure, have been averted had not the Government so persistently, and expensively even, attempted to make it a farming country—something that it was never adapted by nature to be, and which all the enterprise and capital of the world will never make it to be.

But let us return to the special class referred to in this chapter, viz., gentlemen settlers, who are not to be confounded in the peculiarities of their character, hardships, and, too often, failures, with the great mass of other settlers in this country, many of whom, as I have intimated, have, by unremitting personal toil, frugality and practical intelligence, succeeded fairly well, though they are far from constituting the majority even of their own class—what has been the too common result of all their labors, hopes and ambitions? From what I have said, it can be readily understood. In innumerable cases it has simply been carving out a home to starve in. After waiting and toiling and spending for years, they have been compelled, by absolute necessity, to desert their clearings and seek other modes of livelihood. Happy were they if they resolved to do so before their last dollar was spent. In some cases they have clung to the place to the very last, until, actually, they had not the means to carry them away. and, had it not been for that kind Providence which often comes to man's assistance, when all human help has failed, they would have perished from absolute starvation in their homes. A most striking instance of this nature came under my own observation:

One day I entered a dwelling for the purpose of getting something to eat; I had been walking for several hours, and was yet many miles from my destination, and felt quite ready for a good dinner. On stating who I was and preferring my request, I saw at once that the lady of the house was considerably embarrassed, and saw at the same time that I had met with one of the very class whom I am describing. Everything about betokened extreme poverty; but unmistakable evidence of former prosperity and gentility were still there. An old mahogany arm-chair of the most costly workmanship was standing in the corner, and a few more relics of past affluence could be seen. The tone of voice, and manner too, of her I was addressing were those of a perfect lady, and were strikingly reflected in the general deportment of the ragged, hungry-looking children about her; the husband was absent on some business. I felt sorry I had intruded, but I had to make the best of it now. As I was begging of her not to put herself about and give me anything that was convenient, I observed her going to an old clock, which had once been a handsome and costly ornament, and taking from some receptacle a gold coin, and calling her son, a boy of about twelve, she slipped it into his hand and gave him a message, in which I could distinguish something about going to the neighbors. I divined at once what it was: she had nothing decent to offer me to eat, and was sending him to the nearest neighbor to buy something to put before me. When the boy had left the house she could no longer restrain her feelings, and bursting into tears she exclaimed: "Oh, Mr. F——, that is the last guinea of two thousand with which we came to this wretched country, and when it is gone there is nothing that I can see before us but starvation." With the ice thus broken, she told me their whole history. It is needless to recount it here; it was an illustration of what I have been trying to depict, and, alas! not an uncommon nor unfrequent one either.

Some years afterward, being in that locality, I inquired after them, but all I could learn was that the family had been broken up, and deserted the place, but where they had gone or what had become of them only the good Father, who does all things well, knows and cares.

CHAPTER XI.

A Game of Bluff.

THERE is no honester class of men living than shantymen, and the dwellers in the backwoods generally. Trunks and boxes lie about for the most part unlocked, and socks, moccasins, boots, and underclothing are scattered about, or hanging from nails and pegs in every nook and corner of the shanty; and yet every man can always find his own, and seldom or never appropriates the property of another. There is one article, however, which is a notable exception to this honest rule of conduct, and that is liquor of any kind. The shantyman has no conscience in the matter of whiskey. It is considered fair plunder, wherever he can lay his hands on it. If, therefore, you go to the backwoods with a supply of liquor for your private use, you must keep it constantly under lock and key, otherwise it is certain to be pilfered from you before you are a day in the shanty. In the matter of scenting out and appropriating whiskey, the thirsty shantyman is as keen as a weasel, as cunning as a fox, and as unscrupulous as a wolf.

With this exception, however, the general character of the shantymen is one of the strictest probity. A thief is the unknown quantity among them. When, therefore, a robbery does take place in the backwoods, it causes a great flare, and keeps the country in a ferment of excitement for months afterwards. An occurrence of this kind, of the most daring and flagrant character, took place in one of C——'s shanties on the Black River, while I was in that country. This shanty was situated on what was called C——'s upper limit, and during the past and present season has been closed, C—— not deeming it advisable, in the existing state of the lumber market, to carry on active operations there. There was, however, a large quantity of provisions and general shanty goods stored at the place, to be ready for the next winter's work. These were in charge of one man, whose orders were "never to leave the place, except in case of absolute necessity, especially over-night;" and if he required to go to the farm, twenty-five miles distant, on any business, to be sure and obtain a substitute during his absence. And a lonely, weary time he had of it—as we shall presently see; I had had an experience, on a small scale, of this kind of thing myself, and if I found three days of it almost unendurable, what must he have felt it when he had a year and a half of it up to that time, and was bound by contract to remain for another year.

No doubt his only labor was to do his own cooking, and look after the provisions; that is, he had to turn the sacks of flour over from one side to another every now and then, in order to prevent souring, and, during the hot weather, change the brine in the barrels of pork to keep it from rusting; and he could trap and shoot in the vicinity of the shanty as much as he pleased. But, after all he could possibly do, he led a lonely, inactive, dreary life; and as he could not read, and had no internal resources of any kind, and little to occupy his hands, he gradually sank into a kind of mental comatose state. I was told that for days at a time, when he was not sleeping, he would sit gazing at the fire, without sense, or thought, or motion, even the little that he had to do being irksome to him.

When I saw him he looked more like a wild beast than a human being. He had a startled, scared expression on his countenance. When he spoke, which he never did except when addressed, it was in a hurried, abrupt, suspicious tone. My opinion was that by the time he had fulfilled his engagement, he would be quite ready for the lunatic asylum. And no wonder: we talk about the horrors of solitary confinement—here was one of the most trying phases of it that can be conceived of. There would be months at a time when he would never see a human being; his daily and continual life was confined within a comparatively short radius of the shanty. If he could have gone as he pleased, and stayed as he pleased in the woods, it would have been different, but he was practically a prisoner in the deep dungeon of the forest. He was, withal, as the event I am about to relate shows, a man of rare pluck and most active physical energy.

Some imperative business rendered it necessary for him to go to the farm, requiring his absence from the shanty for two days and a night. When he returned, on the evening of the second day, he found the place broken into, and the "van" burst open and plundered.

This "van" is a very peculiar institution of shanty life. It is an immense chest, made of the strongest wood, ribbed with iron bands, and secured by a mighty padlock, of which the foreman and clerk only possess each a key. The van holds all the merchantable goods required for the use of a shanty's gang for a winter's work, viz., pants, socks, flannels, tobacco, medicines, &c., &c. These are given to the men when they want them, and charged to their account. Bouchier, to his terrible consternation, found the "van" in his charge rifled of most of its contents, including some valuable fur of his own trapping; altogether about three hundred dollars' worth **had been taken.**

The poor fellow was, for a little, terribly cast down, and well he might, after all his long, faithful watching, to be duped **at last,** and not only so, but, according to his contract, to have the amount lost deducted from his hard-earned wages; two and a half years' servitude would hardly cover the amount.

But, as was now shown, he was not a man to give **up in despair**; the latent **energy of** his character was **roused, and quickly** finding out **the course the** robber had taken **he determined to** follow him and recover the goods.

Though it **was** after **dark and he** felt greatly fagged with his twenty-five miles tramp from the farm, still **he resolved to** lose no time, but start on the pursuit **at once.** Hastily eating a substantial supper, and putting **a junk of cold pork in** his pocket, he prepared to **set out.** But **at the very outset** he was met by a serious damper. On **examining his** gun, which he had not fired **for several weeks, he** found that it **would not** go off, and, **after trying every** expedient he could think **of, he was totally** unable to extract the damp, rusty charge. Though greatly annoyed he was not deterred from his perilous undertaking, and saying to himself that, "as long as the thief didn't know it wouldn't go off it would serve the purpose just as well," he set out on the track, broad and easily discernible in the loose, soft snow. He had a pretty good idea of the identity of the man whom he was after, having received information at the farm which gave him a clue ; and, if he was right in his conjecture, the fact was not at all reassuring.

It was a man of the name of Gandron—a most notoriously bad character. He was a kind of half-trader, half-trapper and whole savage. He was commonly called the bear in that country. He was known to sleep at the foot of a tree during the coldest nights with a single blanket round him, and could subsist on food which the poorest Indian refused to eat. He was a far larger and stronger man than Bouchier, and a desperado of the purest type. However, Bouchier took up and followed on the track with the fearlessness and pertinacity of a sleuth-hound. I believe that any little latent madness which may have been engendered by his long solitude was now thoroughly awakened in him, and made him completely reckless.

During the whole night he kept steadily on, never

halting for rest or food. Just as day broke he came to an old, deserted shanty, from the chimney of which a thin column of smoke rose, up through the air. Without hesitation he threw open the half-decayed door and stood on the threshold, and, sure enough, there was his man bending over a scanty fire, cooking some f od. As he turned round, at the noise of the opening door, Bouchier thundered in his ear: "give me my goods, or I'll blow your brains out," aiming, as he spoke, his cocked gun direct at his head.

Gandron turned ghastly pale, but as he faced him he suddenly drew a revolver from his belt and half raised it. At the action Bouchier again roared out, "If your raise your hand an inch higher I'll shoot."

It must have been a strange, wild spectacle,—those two fierce, desperate men, facing each other like savage, untamed beasts, in that small shanty, in the lonely solitude of the forest; and none the less so from the absolutely burlesque character of it, for, as it presently turned out, Gandron's revolver was unloaded, nor had he a single cartridge in his pouch. Of course, Bouchier was as ignorant of this fact as Gandron was that the gun was perfectly harmless. It was indeed as pretty a game of bluff as was ever played in human life. But blood will

"A Game of Bluff."

tell. Pluck was to decide the mock duel, and in this Bouchier shewed himself the better man.

Again he thundered out, "If you don't tell me in one second where the goods are, I'll blow your brains out." His resolute tone and fierce, glaring eye gleaming along the cocked gun-barrel struck terror into his antagonist. Gandron thought his last hour was come, and, dropping his hand, he whined out, "I did take the goods, put down your gun, and I'll tell you all about it."

"No, no," said Bouchier, "you don't fool me; throw down your revolver, and come and show me where the goods are."

"Oh, you needn't be frightened," replied the ruffian, "the revolver is not loaded," shewing, as he spoke, the empty chambers.

As Bouchier told me, a great load was at once taken off his heart, and he felt that he could now do as he liked with the fellow. Cautiously stepping aside, and keeping the gun always bearing on his body, he told the man to come out of the shanty and go ahead of him. As Bouchier fully expected, they had not proceeded far on their singular march until the man stopped, and, pointing to a large log a few feet from the track, said sullenly: "Your goods are there, go and get them, and be d—d to you."

But the cunning villain had calculated too much on Bouchier's simplicity. "No, no," said the latter, "bring them out yourself, and be quick about it, or I'll put a ball into you."

With a muttered oath, but knowing he couldn't help himself, the fellow complied, and, going to the spot, brought out parcel after parcel of the stolen goods.

But Bouchier was not done with him yet. Having satisfied himself that nearly all the missing articles were there, he ordered him to make them up into a pack, and, shouldering it, to march on before him to the shanty. With many an imprecation the ruffian was forced to obey, and about mid-day they arrived at the shanty where Bouchier told him to throw down the pack and "be off," pointing out at the same time the course he was to pursue.

The shanty was situated on the edge of a large lake, and on every side of it the trees had all been cut down. Bouchier ordered him to go direct across the lake, and not to stop till he got to the other side, or he would send a ball after him. The man begged hard for some food, saying he was starving, but Bouchier sternly refused, and again threatened him with instant death unless he started that moment. As there was no help for it, the man had to go, and when Bouchier saw him fairly out of sight over the lake he carried the goods inside the shanty, and effectually barring the door, he sank down on the floor in a state of complete and utter exhaustion.

Luckily, in the course of the evening, a trapper with whom he was well acquainted came along, and Bouchier prevailed on him to stay at the shanty while he went the next morning and reported the occurrence at the Farm. It caused, of course, a great noise in the country, but, beyond sending a messenger to the nearest settlements, in order to intercept and arrest the man, if he should make his way in that direction, nothing further was done in the matter.

Some weeks after, however, Gandron was seen at a lumbering depot some distance off, and the party who saw him said that, "with a fearful oath, he declared that if he had only known that Bouchier's gun wouldn't have gone off, he would soon have made mince-meat of him."

Bouchier, as he deserved, received great praise for his plucky and determined conduct, and was for the nonce the hero of the country. He went back to his post, and resumed his lonely vigil, as if nothing very unusual had occurred.

CHAPTER XII.

Keeping House for My Companions.

AS I hinted in my last chapter, I once had the opportunity of enjoying the pleasures of complete solitude in the depths of the forest, and though only for the limited period of three days still it quite satisfied any romantic hankering I might have entertained in that direction, in fact so much so, that I certainly never wish to enjoy it again. I merely lug in the reminiscence here, achronistic as it is, for the benefit of any of my young readers who may be afflicted with a mania of this kind; and, if the reading of it will only do them one-tenth part of the good that the actual experience of it did me in the way of cure, I am sure they will never wish to try it for themselves.

It happened in this wise: On one of my excursions to the Black River country north of the Ottawa I had been staying for some time with two French Canadians, Steve and Xavier, hunting moose and trapping the otter and beaver. Noble fellows they were, too, particularly Steve, who had been my faithful friend and companion in many a glorious tramp, and trapping excursion through the untrodden forests of those vast northern wilds.

Some weeks before that, Steve had shot a very large moose at a considerable distance from the camp, and, as they were getting short of provisions, I could see that they were desirous of going and bringing in the meat, so I offered to stay and keep house for them while they were absent. The alacrity with which they accepted of my offer showed how much they appreciated and valued it. This may sound somewhat singular after what I have said about the generally honest character of backwoods people, and particularly when their hut stood in such a thoroughly isolated, secluded position. But so it was, nevertheless. Roguery is not a product of civilization, nor confined to the towns and settlements. It is indigenous to the soil of human nature, and crops out everywhere and in every grade of human life. In fact, man by nature is a thief, however much he may disguise his thievish propensities under the specious metaphysical name of acquisitiveness, and though its actual outcome may not be so marked and common among the backwoodsmen as elsewhere, still it has to be watched and guarded against even here, and perhaps among no class of these more specially so than the trappers. We have said that shantymen have no conscience about stealing whiskey or liquor in any shape when it is in their reach, so trappers seem to have very little conscience about fur—they intrude on each other's grounds and rob the traps and re-set them again most carefully, in most deliberate and wanton style, and when opportunity offers will even pilfer the dressed hides, apparently without a scruple. And so the trapper has always to be on his guard as to his fur property, both about his camp and in the traps—hence the "chum" business. They always trap in couples—not only for the sake of companionship and mutual assistance, but with the view of having one always at home taking care of things there, while the other is away, perhaps for days at a time, looking after the traps.

My offer, then, to my friends was most opportune and acceptable. It was one of those occasions in which it was necessary they should both go, as it takes two men to skin and dress a moose properly, especially when it is in a frozen state; and, on account of the distance they had to go, they would require to be absent three days—and when we remember that they had about four hundred dollars worth of furs in and about the place, their whole worldly wealth, in fact, we can easily understand how gladly they embraced my offer of mounting guard and holding the fort during their absence.

So next morning they started, each man dragging behind him a large toboggan on which the meat was to be loaded.

I would have much preferred going in the place of one of them, but this was a work which would tax to the uttermost their endurance and strength, and carrying a pack or drawing a load is not my *forte* in the backwoods—it may be very good for developing muscle, but there is not much sport in it—so I was left alone to put in the time the best way I could, until their return.

Though the hut was warm and cosy in itself, yet its surroundings were dreary in the extreme. It was in the heart of the densest forest I had yet seen, over which the silence of the tomb reigned, and in which not a living thing could be seen or heard. There was no game, large or small, in its immediate vicinity, and I did not care, nor indeed was it safe, to go any great distance off in pursuit of it.

It was too dark to read in the hut with any degree of comfort, except by the light of the fire, and this at the best is unsatisfactory work, especially with very small print, as was the case with my two inseparable companions, my Bible and Shakespeare. However, the first day passed off easily enough. I had been having some very heavy exertion the few days previous, and felt considerably fagged, and so managed to do an immense amount of sleeping, and lazy dozing. The cooking was what bothered me the most. This part of my education has been sadly neglected in my youth. I make a good enough dish of tea, but a fearful mess of every other department of the fine art.

But when the darkness of night closed around me it was awfully lonely. Though you know there is not the slightest danger from man or beast, or any other being, still a strange, lonesome, undefinable kind of dread will creep into your heart, and chill the blood. The spirit of loneliness seems to embody itself into shape and sit beside you. Memory, which is not always a pleasant companion, will conjure up black and ugly reminiscences. All that is eerie and awesome in silence and darkness seems floating around you. You sit spell-bound and motionless, almost afraid to breathe or stir, least you should arouse and anger some invisible, unearthly and unknown evil. Unconsciously you find yourself looking fearfully around into the dark corners, and at the unbarred door behind you. The thought that some hideous monster will silently open it, and noiselessly walk in, will possess you, and though you will not yield to place a log against it, still you think there is no harm in taking your double-barrel down from the pegs above it, and placing it in a more convenient position, and, unwittingly also, you cast a side glance at the big axe to see if it is handy. And then you suddenly laugh aloud at your fears and precaution, and even get up and dance about, and shout hilariously as if it were all a capital joke, and too comical for anything. But it's no go! This counterfeit merriment and steamed-up courage soon evaporate, and the dark shades will again insidiously creep into, and overshadow the soul. I don't profess to be either a braver or more timid man than the ordinary run of mortals, but there is a something peculiar in these surroundings which weighs down and oppresses the spirits, and makes a coward of you after all. One thing I do know, that I would rather a thousand times, when I am alone in the depths of the forest, spend the night in the open air, where I can see the stars and the trees on every side, than in the snuggest and strongest hut that was ever built.

However, the night passed slowly away, and with the bright, glad morning **came that** lightness of heart, and boldness of spirit which **are** always engendered by robust, vigorous health, **and highstrung**, overflowing animal life.

After breakfast, also, I had work to do. I must chop fire-wood. So, **shouldering the** big axe, I sallied forth in quest of a proper tree to fell.

The uninitiated in these matters will, no doubt, wonder why there should be any searching at all for **fuel** when the dense forest is **at the** very door, **and all around you.** But the fact is that it is often a very difficult matter to come across just the right kind of wood **for** burning. The forest is composed not only of green, but also, **for** the most part, **of** soft wood, which, in winter especially, is quite unfit for fuel. **The** great object is to get a dead, dry tamarac, this, combined with green birch, makes a capital **fire for every** purpose.

I **soon came** across the tree I wanted, and went at it **most lustily. I am no** great hand at the axe, but I **am better at it** than the saucepan anyway. So the tree soon began to **totter,** and its lofty top **to** bend over; almost mechanically, **I** stepped a little **to the** side. *If I had not taken that step, this book would never have* ***been written.*** In falling, the top of the tree struck against a smaller one, causing the severed trunk to fly back from the stump; it whizzed past me, within an inch of my side, with the velocity of a cannon ball, and buried itself deep in the snow beyond. It was a narrow escape. If it had struck me it would have crushed in my chest like an egg-shell. For a little while I stood perfectly paralyzed. I think in all my life I was never so near death as at that moment. My first thought, *when I could think*, was deep, profound gratitude to the Almighty for His interposing hand; the most fervent *Thank God!* fell from my lips that I had ever uttered; and good cause had I for it. If I had not been killed outright I would have been so maimed that I could not have stirred from the spot, and would have lain there until my companions found me, if I could have survived the cold and exposure so long.

There are perhaps more men killed in the woods in this way than in any other. The butt of the tree is almost certain to fly from the stump, and the course it may take is often uncertain, though it can generally be known by watching the top.

It was some time before I could muster sufficient resolution to proceed with my work, and when I did, it was with such fear and trepidation that I was heartily glad when it was over, and I found myself safely back within the walls of the hut. Such was the shock my nerves received at the time that it was many months before I fully recovered from it. Often I would awaken in the middle of the night, in a cold perspiration, and with a great shudder as the remembrance of my narrow escape flashed upon me in my sleep. I have never attempted to fell a tree since.

The rest of the day, and that night, passed away drearily enough. I never was so heartily sick of a business as I was of that housekeeping.

The next morning, while casting about in my mind for something to divert myself with, it occurred to me to try my hand at cooking a beaver tail for my dinner. I had heard it said that "a man never knows what he can accomplish until he is cast upon his own resources," so I thought this was a famous opportunity to test the virtue of the old maxim.

There were three tails stuck into a chink in the wall opposite to me; selecting one of these I pondered how I was to proceed. The tail was hard and dry as a shingle, so I thought the best thing to do was to parboil it first in hot water, and then fry it in the gridiron in pork grease, which is the universal substitute for butter in the backwoods. So this I did, taking my leisure, and "doing it up brown" as I thought. Then, with all the concomitants of potatoes, "scones" and tea, I sat down in great expectation of a right royal dinner.

But the first mouthful I took of that beaver tail was something never to be forgotton. It was simply horrible. Of all the nauseating, abominable, disgusting morsels I ever tasted that was the worst. I can compare it with nothing uneatable under the sun. Putrid carrion fried in rancid lard couldn't be worse. Though I instantly spat it out in disgust, yet the sickening flavor of it seemed to penetrate my whole system like prussic acid, and I haven't got the taste of it out of my mouth to this day.

In a rage I kicked the dish into the fire, and bolted for the open air. I had had enough of dinner for that day, and resolved I would cook no more till my companions came back, though I should fast for a week.

Towards evening they returned, dragging enormous loads of meat after them. They could not have had less than four hundred pounds weight, besides the hide, which would weigh fully fifty more.

They were greatly concerned when they heard of my narrow escape with the tree, the peril of which they fully understood and appreciated.

However, all's well that ends well, and we spent our last night together in the most enjoyable and hilarious manner, and often awoke the sleeping echoes, and made the solemn old forest about us ring again with our shouts and songs of uproarious merriment.

CHAPTER XIII.

About Deer Shooting.

THERE is no more enjoyable excursion in the world than for a party of kindred spirits to start off on a deer-shooting expedition to our far backwoods. The very preparation for it is in itself a delight. You love to ponder over and calculate every detail and arrangement. You rack your invention to find out new and approved articles and expedients for promoting your pleasure, comfort and success in the hunt. If you are flush of money your extravagance in purchasing supplies of all necessary and unnecessary articles will be beyond all bounds. Your grocer and gunsmith are quite ready to gratify every whim, and are prolific of suggestions of the most useless, cumbersome, and absurd *comforts* and *contrivances*.

Perhaps a word here from me as to my experience, and what I think makes up the best outfit for such an excursion, may not be out of place.

Some of the most pleasant reminiscences of my life are connected with deer shooting, and its accompanying sports, far back amid the glorious scenery of our backwoods lakes. Without doubt I have had most delightful excursions, and for an amateur have generally been fairly successful in my sport. And I ascribe my pleasure and success in a very large degree to the *personnel* of the party who accompanied me on these excursions. And this I would lay down as the very first element to be considered in arranging for a deer-shooting expedition. If your companions are not congenial, or not of the right stamp in every sense, far better not to go at all, or at least with no companion but your dog, and your servant.

Now, there are three classes of fellows that I utterly detest to be with in the woods; first those who go on a trip of this kind merely for the sake of having a " grand spree." They must have a cartload of wine and beer and liquors with them, and from morning until night, and from the time they leave till they get back, it is just one everlasting "swipe." These men are not only a nuisance and an encumbrance, but also a source of continual danger to themselves and all around them. There is a certain amount of peril attendant upon all these trips. In crossing some of our broad lakes in a small bark canoe, particularly if the wind is at all high, you require to be cool, collected, and steady as a rock. And if you are following deer you require especially to have all your wits about you. If a man is in liquor he runs a great risk of upsetting and losing his rifle, perhaps his life too, or of shooting his companion, or at least of missing the deer to a certainty, and spoiling the morning's hunt. In every way, both in the camp and on the hunt, these fellows are not only useless, but positive spoilers of sport for all about them.

Another class that I can't abide are those *dilettante*, pernickety sort of fellows who must have all their little comforts and luxuries, and toilet apparatus, and other nicknacks about them. They must carry their combs and brushes, their sponges and night-shirts, and all the thousand and one appurtenances of their home life with them. They are awfully nice about the cooking and washing of the dishes, arranging of the beds, &c., and in fact in many ways are simply a pest about the camp. They make everybody thoroughly uncomfortable and nervous, and impress you with a sense of inferiority in the scale of social life and respectability. They are a kind of living rebuke to your own negligence in these matters, and say to you, as plainly as if they put it in so many words, "you are one of the great unwashed." Oh, how I abominate these fellows! I feel as if kicking was too good for them. I would rather have a dirty Hottentot with me than one of these nice gentlemen. It is one everlasting grumble with them about trivial inconveniences and discomforts. Equally with the last class, they are perfect kill-joys about the camp, and to be avoided as you would the plague. I have had my experience of these chaps, and I hope a kind Providence will save me from ever having it again.

There is a third class of men to whom I also object as companions in the hunt, though they are not nearly so objectionable as the two former, viz., those who make a toil and a burden out of the excursion, instead of a pleasure and relaxation. They are the men who go in for hard work and take a pride in the mere "roughing it." They are just the very antithesis of the last class, and, though you have a kind of respect for them, still in many ways they are a nuisance and a detriment to your comfort and enjoyment. They will have you off to bed at dark and up in the morning long before day-light, and keep you shivering round the fire hours before it is necessary. They are great at chopping, cooking, and carrying, and are everlastingly busy at something. As you lie at your ease, placidly smoking your cutty before the fire, your ears are dinned with the most opprobrious epithets—lazy-bones, sleepy-heads, sluggards, &c.—until you almost feel ashamed of your very existence. Now I don't believe in this sort of thing at all. When I go on a trip of this kind, I want to enjoy myself, and have as little toil and drudgery as I can possibly help. If you can't afford to have servants with you, then of course you have to work, do all the work in fact,—and toilsome and dirty work it often is. But I don't believe in working merely for work's sake, and as a kind of bravado and show-off of your knowledge and experience in these matters. Let each man attend to his own business in the camp, let the servants do the work for which they are engaged and paid, and let us eat, drink, smoke, hunt and be merry. No fear but we shall get plenty of muscular exercise to keep us in "good twist," without doing any works of supererogation.

But with the *personnel* of the camp made up of right good fellows, who thoroughly understand one another, and who are determined, come what may, not to grumble or complain, or quarrel with one another—in a word, to act on the M. T. principle of being jolly in all circumstances—you have, at the very outset, the prime essential of solid comfort and enjoyment throughout your whole trip.

Now, as to the material outfit, a great deal could be said and written, and I might content myself and the reader by simply saying, take with you nothing but what is absolutely necessary; but still a few hints in this direction may not be amiss. With regard to clothes, one suit of heavy rough tweed, with one change of under-clothes and three or four pairs of socks, is quite sufficient. A soft felt hat is the best of all headgear, far better than any kind of cap —a Scotch cap particularly, which so many affect, is a piece of jaunty discomfort and inconvenience. Top boots of light leather reaching to the knee are the best for every season of the year, and, take them all in all, are the most suitable foot garb for the bush, also a pair of strong leather slippers for the camp; the latter answer capitally, too, for wearing in the canoe when you are after deer, and, in case of upsetting, are less encumbrance in swimming. Many a man has been drowned in attempting to draw off his heavy top-boots in the water, for it is impossible to swim any length of time with them on.

A long roomy oilskin coat reaching below the top of the boots, is indispensable, it will keep you dry and comfortable in the heaviest rain, and is besides a famous thing at night to spread over you if the weather is either damp or cold. Special attention should be paid to the coat, one of the right kind adds greatly to the hunter's comfort and convenience. I had one which I wore for many years, and I can't tell you the satisfaction I got out of that coat. It was of a greyish-green color, of coarse, strong tweed, and had no less than sixteen pockets in it. I could easily carry a dozen partridges in it without being the least impeded in walking through the bush, thus obviating the need of a game-bag, that pest and encumbrance to the hunter in thick woods and swamps. The best model of a hunting coat that I have yet seen is made by J. D. Anderson, St. James street, Montreal. It is a most becoming thing, and, at the same time, contains within it every carrying convenience for game, ammunition, and "snack," which a hunter requires for a day's tramp through the bush.

As to the provisions that should be taken, every one must consult his own taste and means. If you are going to camp permanently on one spot during the whole time of your holidays, then take everything and anything your stomach may desire, from potted goose's liver up to Westphalian sugar-cured hams. But my experience in this prog and grog business is that, after a few days in the keen, bracing, oxygenated atmosphere of the backwoods, I get to have a perfect distaste for these delicacies and luxuries which a petted, pampered appetite rejoices in amid the artificialties and refinements of so-called cultured and high-toned life. My stomach comes to care for nothing but strong meat; anything less seems to be an imposition and an insult to it, and is repudiated with contempt. Fat pork, bacon, fresh beef, venison, game of all kinds, strong tea, bread, potatoes and onions served up on tin-plates, and in bountiful abundance, are what the appetite craves for and revels in. As for liquors, I consider Jamaica rum the best for the woods; it is sufficiently exhilarating for all convivial purposes, and has besides a staying power in it that no other spirit possesses. If you wish to know my opinion on this liquor question just skip over to the end of this chapter, and you will find there in full what I have already written in "Three Months among the Moose" on this point.

If, however, in your excursion you expect to have a great deal of moving about from place to place, and, consequently, very considerable portaging and carrying, then, I beseech you, for mercy's sake, to remember the poor canoesmen and cook, and cut down your *impedimenta* to the narrowest compass and the lightest weight. Nothing these men detest more than to carry loads of **useless** superfluous baggage. If you have much of this sort of work **to do, you** will find that what is just necessary for your comfort and pleasure is **amply** sufficient for them and you to transport.

Of course one of the most important items in the outfit is the **gun** business. I am **often** asked what is the best shooting-piece to take to the backwoods. **Of rifles the** Ballard is my **favorite.** After an experience of nearly **twenty** years, and during that time having handled almost every new and approved patent that has come out, I still retain my preference for this piece. It is of simple, yet strong mechanism, and of long range; and if you can adapt the sights, either by filing or altering, to suit your own eye, then you have the most accurate precision of **aim of any** piece I know. I am speaking now of the genuine first-class Ballard, **not** of those pot-metal things which go by that name, and which you can buy from $5 up to $17. However, there are so many new and excellent styles of rifles coming out continually, that it is difficult to dogmatise on this point. Every one has his favorite, and what suits one eye may not another.

A double-barrelled breach-loader, a revolver, a hunting-knife and a drinking-cup, and your sporting accoutrement is complete. I go to Costen's, Montreal, when I want anything in this line. Both brothers are practical, experienced sportsmen, both with fish and game, as well as thorough gunsmiths. Their establishment is one of the most varied and extensive in Canada.

Our outfit is now complete; we are thoroughly equipped *cap-à-pie*, and so, hurrah, with a merry heart, for the far backwoods!

Our destination is some one of the innumerable lakes which lie far inland in Central Ontario, between the Madawaska and Mississippi. It is comparatively an easy matter to reach these places now, compared with what it used to be. The Canadian Pacific on the one side, and the Kingston and Pembroke Railway, on the other, will take you to a point from which, with a waggon, you can go to any place where you have decided to make your camp and head-quarters. The Kingston and Pembroke for a long distance traverses a country that is yet so wild and unbroken that, in many localities, within a mile of it, you can pitch your tent on the shore of some small lake in perfect solitude and isolation, and, if the place be judiciously selected, have as good deer-hunting and shooting of small game, as the heart of man can desire.

Without further delay or explanation, we will

transport ourselves **at once to the** lonely, retired and delightful banks of Middle Branch Lake, and there we will pitch our tent, and make ourselves happy for a month to come.

This lake gets its name from being the fountain head of the middle branch of the Clyde River, the North and South branch being on either side. It is a beautiful lake, with grand picturesque surroundings. Tiny islets **stud its surface, and deep bays fissure its shores;** these often extend a mile or more inward, and terminate in the most lovely vistas. On one side of the lake stand beautiful groves of yellow poplar, white birch, and umbrageous balsam, where the partridge loves to **feed** and play ; another side is all reedy marsh, and dense boggy swamp, **where** duck and rabbit abound ; **and the third stretches away** in unbroken solitude **in a vast forest of** gigantic pine and hemlock, with here **and there** almost impenetrable jungles of cedar **and** spruce—the home of **the deer,** the bear and the wolf.

Into **the** depths of this forest our huntsmen will lead the dogs, and **the first fresh** track of a deer they scent they will instantly give chase upon, and with **loud** and fierce " tongue " will waken up the sleeping **echoes** of the forest, and make it ring again with **their** uproarious clamor. The panic-stricken deer will bound in every direction, and circle round and round in the bush, in the vain attempt to tire out and escape from his merciless pursuers, until finally, in despair, hearing the loud baying coming nearer and nearer, and the hounds rapidly closing upon him, he will head straight for the lake, and, after pausing for a moment on its brink to assure himself that the enemy is still on his track, will plunge headlong into its cool waters. But, alas; poor brute, his instinct has failed to warn him that he has only escaped from one enemy to fall into the power of more deadly and unsparing ones, who, if their skill and coolness are only equal to their opportunity, will soon put an end to his gallant career.

Our chapter has lengthened itself out to an unreasonable extent, and, as we shall see some of the details and exciting pleasures of this sport in those which immediately follow, we will bring it to a close, with this remark, that, notwithstanding all that has been said and written about the cruelty and butchery of this sport, and a great deal more nonsense to the same effect, we hold that it is the most enjoyable and exciting, as it it also the fairest and most sportsmanlike, mode of hunting deer of any that is adopted in the backwoods. In this respect it stands far ahead of still-hunting, that is, tracking the deer in the snow till you overtake and shoot him; or, lying in wait for him on the runaway as he is chased by the dogs—for the deer has special paths in the woods in which they always run when pursued, and which are well known to the hunter—when he sometimes comes so close to you as you crouch behind tree or rock, that you can touch him with the muzzle of your gun; or, lastly, of shooting him by the jack-light after night by the marshy side of river or lake where he comes to drink, or escape from the torments of flies and mosquitoes. In these three last modes, there is hardly any escape for the deer, if only ordinary coolness and patience are exercised. But in watering the deer with hounds there are far more "let out" of the lake, and escape with their lives than are shot and killed in it; and it is a sport that is attended with much more danger to the hunter than any of the others, and is not this the very essence and soul of true sport all the world over?

"I have often been asked the question whether, in such circumstances (camping out in winter), it is a good thing to use freely, or even moderately, alcoholic spirits. My answer is, emphatically, no. I believe that a draught of good whiskey, that is high wines diluted with water (for high wines is the only liquor you can carry in that country, where every pound's weight is to be considered) is an excellent thing when you are thoroughly chilled, wet and fagged out. I think it assists nature to recuperate, and is generally beneficial in such cases, provided the quantity taken is moderate. But to take it when you are going to sleep, with the idea that it will keep up the heat of the body, or under *ordinary* circumstances in winter backwoods travelling, is a foolish and dangerous mistake. The true theory of the question as given to me by one of our most eminent physicians is this: "alcohol except in moderate quantity, although from its irritating effect on the nerves of the stomach, and its stimulating influence upon the circulation, it produces the subjective feeling of warmth, really lowers the temperature of the blood. This effect is thought to depend upon a depressive influence exerted by the alcohol upon the cells of the body, and upon a temporary paralysis of the blood vessels. This paralysis is followed by a larger circulation of blood in the superficial blood-vessels, and consequently greater radiation of heat from the surface, while the depressing action of the spirit in the cells diminishes the combustion of the body and, *pro tanto*, the production of heat."

On the other hand, strong tea and fat pork, besides having a stimulating and heating effect at the time, possess a staying power behind, which has a most beneficial effect in warding off and neutralizing the effects of extreme cold. Take it all in all, I think that a man with an ordinarily strong and healthy physique is just as well without alcohol, in any form, in the backwoods, even in the depths of winter, than with it. But this is a matter very much of experience and constitution. Mere conscientious scruples have nothing to do with it in such circumstances.

CHAPTER XIV.

A Ride on a Deer's Back in the Lake.

ONE morning Jim and I started off in our "fathom and a half" bark canoe to watch a part of the lake in which we fully expected the deer would be watered by the dogs.

It was a glorious morning in October, which, to my mind, is the most delightful month in the year for backwoods sport. The weather then is generally sufficiently bracing to make vigorous exercise an agreeable recreation, and not too cold to make it unpleasant to lie in ease and comfort in the open air. The woods, too, are clothed in their most beautiful dress. The autumn tints and colors are in their full ripeness of mellow golden glory. Every possible hue and shade of prismatic radiance is displayed in grand effulgence. Every reed and shrub, and plant and tree has its own distinctive and peculiar coloring, and each seems to rival the other in its showy finery. All Nature seems to be out for a gala-day in holiday attire.

As we glided swiftly over the bright waters of the lake, just lit up with the golden glory of the rising sun, our hearts beat in unison with the bright and gorgeous surroundings. The lake itself was beautifully embosomed in a magnificent framework of yellow and purple and gold, studded every here and there with bold jutting cliffs of whitey-gray limestone. From our point of observation we could take in the whole lake, which was about a mile and a half long and a mile wide. In the clear, bracing translucent atmosphere every object stood out in bright sunny relief, and presented one of those scenes of loveliness which are photographed for ever upon the memory.

Suddenly, the deep baying of the hounds broke upon our ears, faintly echoing through the intervening forest, and after continuing for a while, gradually died away as the chase took another direction.

There is a strange wild charm in this sweetest of all music, at least to the hunter's ears. Now it swells out in clear triumphant tone, as if the hounds felt quite sure of their prey, and were just upon him. Then a quick angry yelp will tell as plainly as human speech that they are at fault in the scent and the deer is escaping them. But again it will ring out clearer and fuller, and unmistakably nearer and nearer. There is no doubt of it the deer has given up his winding and circling in the bush and is "heading" straight for the lake, with the hounds "full tongue" after him. Hastily taking our places in the canoe, for up to this time we had been sitting at our ease on the bank, we shoved off a few yards and watched intently the shore line of the lake in the direction of the approaching chase. Jim, who is a first-class canoeman, seated himself in the stern, and I took the bow, with a rifle and the double-barreled gun charged with heavy buckshot.

It is always the rule in this sport that the man in the bow does the shooting, and the one in the stern the steering and main part of the paddling. This is an excellent rule, and should always be adhered to, and this for two reasons: first, in following the deer the steersman cannot shoot without great danger to the bowman, with whom he is generally in a line with the deer; and, secondly, he has quite enough to do in directing the course of the canoe, and keeping it steady at the moment the other fires.

The deer in taking the water is often very capricious in the spot he chooses for his plunge. So it proved in this case. Instead of entering where the loud baying led us to expect, he seems to have run along the shore for a distance, and plunged in far up the lake, more than a mile away.

Though we couldn't hear the plunge yet Jim's hawk eye detected the splashing of the water in the dazzling glittering of the sun's rays, and, hastily exclaiming, "there he is," headed the canoe in that direction, and away we dashed down the lake. Now is the time for coolness and lake craft. It would never do to paddle too close to the animal, else he will see us too soon, and, re-entering the woods, give the dogs another chase to some other lake, and our sport would be spoiled for the day. We must give him time to swim fairly out into the lake, and then dash upon him and head him off from the shore.

The deer as soon as he plunges into the water will lie perfectly motionless for a little, and with ears lying back on his neck will listen for the approaching dogs. If he judges that they are still on his track and pressing him closely he will start out for the opposite shore,—so it turned out in this case. But Jim and I, like some righteous people we read of, had been cautious overmuch. Miscalculating the distance the deer had to swim to the further shore, we had waited too long, and allowed him to get too good a start of us, and, though we "laid into" our paddles with all our might, and made our light canoe fairly bound over the water, still we were more than a hundred yards behind him when he reached the shore. Quickly dropping my paddle I seized the rifle and fired just as he rose from the water. But my violent paddling and the dancing of the canoe made my aim unsteady, and after following his track some distance through the woods, and seeing no marks of blood we came to the humiliating conclusion that we had ignominiously missed and lost him. Vastly annoyed, and mightily out of conceit with ourselves and thinking the game was all up for that day, we returned to the canoe ; but just as we were stepping into it Jim's keen eye sighted another chap just leaving the shore opposite the point from which we had come, more than a mile away.

Without waiting to reload the rifle, as my trusty double-barrel was ready at my hand, again we dashed away at high-pressure speed up the lake. That was a paddle, indeed, with a vengeance. If it had been for sweet life we couldn't have paddled harder. With every muscle strained to its utmost tension we went at it, resolved not to be too late this time. And the deer gave us all we could do. The moment he saw us he redoubled his efforts, and made for the shore at a tremendous speed. And these fellows can swim when they are put to it. Under the first impulse of their fright they almost leap out of the water; they raise swells behind them like a steamboat, and dash ahead at an amazing rate. But they cannot keep it up, they soon tire; it is impossible for them to maintain this pace, and after the first dash the light canoe, under the quick powerful sweeps of the paddle, rapidly gains upon them. When we came within a dozen yards of him I raised the gun, and, while Jim steadied the canoe, I fired straight for the back of his head, but a miss is as good as a mile, and, though I riddled his ear with the shot, yet, instead of crippling, it only maddened him into more strenuous exertions for escape. But I felt we had him safe enough yet. I had another barrel left, and he was yet a considerable distance from the shore; so, dropping the gun, I again seized the paddle, and again we bore rapidly down upon him. I knew there must be no miss this time, so reserving my fire until we were full broadside of him, and not twenty feet off, I raised the gun and fired right into his heaving flank. Fired, forsooth! Perdition seize all muzzle-loaders, and this one in particular! The cap only snapped, and, as far as the charge was concerned, the deer might laugh in our beards. Another yard or two and he would reach a long dead pine that had fallen out into the lake, and once over it he was safe, and, like his brother at the other end of the lake, would soon show us a clean pair of heels into the woods, for, of course, the log was an effectual barrier to our canoe. I took all this in in a moment, and also the humiliation and disgrace of the thing: within the space of a quarter of an hour to miss and let two deer out of the lake. What a tale to go back to camp with! Presto! It shall not be. I suddenly seemed to be possessed with the rage and fury of ten devils, and, without a thought of the consequences, I sprang from the canoe, with the agility of a gorilla, right on to the back of the deer, and clasped him round the shoulders with my arms. It was the act of a madman, as I quickly discovered. The deer, for a moment or two, continued on in his plunging career, confounded by the strange rider on his back, but only for a moment. The savage instinct of the animal asserted itself. It was a spike-horn buck, the most dangerous of all the deer family, when cornered up and at bay. He evidently felt himself in this position now, and suddenly giving his shoulders a violent heave, he threw me backwards into the water, and, before I could recover myself, he wheeled round, quick as lightning, and struck me with his forehoof with all his terrible strength, fair on the breast, and sent me down like a piece of lead to the bottom of the lake. The moment my head reappeared at the surface, he went into me with his horns. I saw at once that he had no intention of escaping, but was bound to make mince-meat of me on the spot. And, somehow or other, the demon of battle got possession of me, too, so at it we went, full tilt; it was a do-or-die understanding that was instantaneously arrived at between us. Just as his sharp un-antlered horn was about to immolate me, my right hand, with that quickness and precision which come in such straits, we know not how, grasped it with the clutch of desperation, and my left, at the same time, unconsciously I believe, seized his right leg, just at the fetlock. If I had studied the manœuvre for an hour I couldn't have got a more advantageous hold of him. I felt this instinctively, and held on and grappled with him with the fury, and the strength of despair.

From early experience and long training I always feel perfectly at home in the water, and it served me well now. With a sudden exertion of strength, and, I suppose, what wrestlers would call a "contrip sleight," I threw his buckship fairly on his back, at the same time falling myself between his legs.

Then it was that the brute in turn shewed his skill, and gave me what the pugilists style a tremendous "left-hander." Suddenly drawing up his hind legs, he dug his sharp hoofs into my chest, and ripped and tore down with mad fury. I felt my watch-guard, pants, drawers, everything give way before them. The pain was excruciating. I thought my last hour was come, and yelled most lustily for Jim to help me, though I never thought for a moment of giving up or letting go my hold. Jim, by this time, had got out of the canoe and run up the log, and leaning out as far as he could towards the scene of combat, made a lunge with his long hunting knife at the deer's throat; the glittering blade whizzed past within a hair's-breadth of my own jugular, as we plunged about on every side, and, telling him to let me alone, at it we went, pell-mell again. Sometimes I would be under him, and again I would get him below me, and then his ripping and tearing would be repeated. I suppose we had been at it for ten minutes or more, when, with a violent twist, I threw myself across his neck, and held his head under the water with his open gasping mouth upwards; the water poured down his throat in torrents, and, after a terrible gurgling and spasm, he lay perfectly still, dead, drowned, beneath me. It was over at last, and I was the conqueror of the spike-horn.

But, all joking aside, it was a narrow escape for me. It was a touch-and-go sort of business all through. If I hadn't drowned him he would have drowned or killed me to a certainty, for he was fairly crazed with the fury of despair, and when maddened there is not a more dangerous and determined brute than the spike-horn buck. He is called spike-horned because he has no antlers. His horns are like those of a bull, straight and sharp-pointed. When we dragged him up on the log, the outer rind of his horn where I had seized him, came off like a husk of corn, showing how firm was the grip I had of him.

But our adventure for the day was not over yet. On coming alongside the deer, when my gun snapped, we had been going at such a speed that after I leaped from the canoe Jim was unable to stop it, and the impetus drove it upon the log with such a force as to stove a hole through the bottom. In the excitement of the time we never noticed this until we were out in the lake on our way to the camp. Then the water began to pour in, and though we paddled with all our might to the shore, it filled so rapidly that we were a considerable distance from it when the canoe suddenly sank under us, and we found ourselves struggling in the water. There was nothing for it but to swim for the shore, which was quite a pull in our heavy clothes. I had had enough of adventure for the day, so Jim took his share, and divesting himself of his clothes, he swam out and brought canoe, guns and deer all safe to the land. The canoe had not upset, for as soon as relieved of our weight it had risen to the surface. We soon caulked up the hole, and arrived without further mishap at the camp, where we were feasted and lionized by our companions for the rest of the day.

The obstinate bull-dog ferocity of the deer, when thoroughly at bay, is a well-known characteristic of the animal all the world over, but nowhere I believe is it more strongly brought out than in these backwoods of ours. In other circumstances, the invariably timorous nature of the deer is apt to deceive the unwary hunter, and lead him into too close quarters with him, when he ought rather to have kept a respectful distance. To approach, and especially lay hold on a deer when he is in a tight place, is a most foolish and dangerous experiment. It can be done only with great risk to life or limb.

I could illustrate this by a dozen stirring encounters with the animal, which I have heard and known to be authentic, but one will suffice for the present. In this case, however, the gentleman did not escape so well as I did, but, in consequence of the injuries he received, has become a helpless cripple, and partially paralyzed for life.

He was a gentleman settler belonging to one of the most respectable families in Canada, and had obtained a patent for a block of land on one of the Trout Lakes, which, at that time, more than twenty years ago, was in the heart of the dense virgin forest. He was a keen sportsman, of a powerful athletic frame, and at the time we refer to was not more than twenty-one years of age.

One night, late in the Fall, he was returning home to his lonely location from the market town of Perth, where he had been with a load of grain. As he was driving merrily along, through the dense pinery, he heard his dog barking furiously at some animal at a distance ahead of him on the road. Arming himself with a big stick, he hurried to the spot, and found the dog fiercely engaged with a large buck which had turned at bay, and was fighting bravely with his assailant. Without hesitation he joined in the *mêlée*, and assaulted the enraged animal with his club. But he soon found out, to his sorrow, that he had miscalculated the issues of the contest. The deer, doubly enraged at the attack of this fresh enemy, became perfectly frantic, and disregarding the dog sprang at him, and with one blow of his powerful fore-foot struck him to the ground, and would soon have gored him to death with his sharp antlers had not the dog fastened his teeth into his haunches and compelled him to desist, and, after a short struggle, to take to flight into the bush. . With great difficulty the gentleman was able to crawl to his sleigh, and proceed homewards. When he arrived at his house he contrived, in a semi-conscious state, to stable the team, and then to creep into his own bed. The farming season being over all his hired men had gone to their several homes, and he was entirely alone on the place.

Four days afterwards one of his men happened to come to the place, and, struck with the strange desolate quietness of everything around, went first to the stables, where he found the horses and cattle nearly perished for want of food and water, and, continuing his search, he found the master of the establishment in his bed, unconscious in the delirium of a raging fever. He immediately went for assistance, and the nearest doctor, more than fifteen miles distant, was sent for. But it was too late. The terrible injuries he had received from the deer, combined with the exposure to cold, and want of attendance in his lonely, fireless house, at that inclement season of the year, had brought on brain fever, and paralysis. Everything that money, kind nursing, and medical skill could give were bestowed upon him, but in vain. For months he lay almost unconscious, and when he partially recovered it was only to find himself a helpless cripple, and his powerful constitution utterly shattered. And though for the past few years he has been able to go about and superintend the affairs of his extensive and valuable farm, still it is only as the wreck, physically, of what he once was.

CHAPTER XV.

"*I'll Teach them how to Shoot Deer.*"

THERE is a great difference between shooting at a target at the rifle ranges, and shooting at deer or any other game in the backwoods. A man may be a crack shot at the former and not worth "chucks" at the latter. Target practice is mainly mechanical, and according to formula, and though peculiarity of eye and steadiness of nerve are conditions of proficiency in it, yet all these are required, and much more too, before a man can be a successful sportsman in the woods or on the water. There is a kind of mental discipline in this sport which tends to improve and sharpen a man's intellectual capacities, quite apart from its muscle and sinew developing effect. A man must have all his wits about him when he goes a-hunting. In fact a genuine live hunt is as good for man's brain as a keenly-contested game of chess. A cool, patient, calculating, well-balanced head, combined with quickness and precision of aim, and supported by a strong, hardy, enduring frame, are the component essentials of the successful hunter.

If a man gets into a "fluster" on the lake, "runaway," or trail, he is done for; he might as well shoot at the deer with his eyes shut, as far as any skill of his is concerned. And if he becomes weak, tired, and out of patience, then it is no longer sport for him, and he had far better return to camp and smoke his pipe in ease and comfort before the fire. And yet there are many people who are goosey enough to suppose that because a man can hit the bull's-eye every time at five hundred yards, he is quite able to knock over a deer at almost any range in the bush. And when you tell them that nine out of every ten deer are shot within a range of eighty or a hundred yards, they laugh to scorn the idea of ever missing one at all. And none are more prone to fall into this error than those target heroes themselves.

We had a most amusing illustration of this at our camp on Park's lake on one occasion. A person, whom we shall call Taylor, had gained a great reputation among the volunteers as a first-class shot, and had carried off several valuable prizes. Taylor was a capital fellow in many ways, but egregiously vain and boastful about his shooting. When he heard that we were going up for a hunt to the woods, he was very anxious to come along with us. Now, we were always very particular as to the parties we invited to go with us on those trips, for if the *personnel* of the party is not to your liking the whole pleasure of the thing may be marred. Yet, lest it might be supposed that we were jealously afraid of Taylor's boasted skill as a shot, we gave him permission to come along. I had a dim suspicion, also, that we might take the conceit out of the fellow before we were done with him. And, in truth, I was very desirous that we should, for it had been told me that he had said, "if I go with them, I'll teach them how to shoot deer."

So after we had got fairly settled in our snug camp, and everything in good working order, Taylor made his appearance, and was received by us with all the respect and deference that his target celebrity was entitled to. Determined that he should make his *début* on the lake with all possible *éclat*, we placed him in our best canoe, and gave him, as steersman, Joe M——, as skilful and experienced a canoesman as ever paddled after deer.

Our camp was situated just on the edge of the lake which they were to watch. I had given up my place to Taylor, and remained at the camp for this run, so that I could have a full view of the anticipated sport.

Sure enough, in about an hour a large buck with magnificent antlers, came plunging into the lake, and Joe, with his usual adroitness, headed it off from the shore, and drove it fair for the middle of the lake. A better chance to shoot a deer was never given to mortal man, and never did mortal man make a more ignominious failure. He kept cool, and stuck to his paddle well enough until he came within nice easy range, about twenty yards or so, and then with his own rifle, that had scored so many bull's-eyes, he fired, and missed. That shot, or its miss, let us charitably suppose, seemed completely to demoralize him. He was suddenly seized with "buck fever" in its most malignant type. Instead of dropping his rifle and plying his paddle in order to regain the lost ground, he popped in another cartridge and fired again, and kept on firing as fast as he could reload. And such wild, wide-of-the-mark firing, I never witnessed before or since; if he had been trying to avoid the animal, he could not have done better. If the prizes had been for misses instead of bull's-eyes, he could have loaded a cart with them. The lake was scored with misses for half a mile on every side of that amazed buck.

In the meantime the animal was rapidly increasing the distance between himself and the boat, and diminishing it in the direction of the shore, for in spite of Joe's most strenuous exertions, it was impossible, unaided, to keep up with him. Every shot that was fired retarded the canoe's speed and was in favor of the deer, and he would certainly have soon escaped, if he had continued straight ahead; but, through some unaccountable freak or other, which these animals will sometimes take in the water, he suddenly turned off at right angles to the course he was pursuing and headed straight up the lake towards the spot where I was standing with old Tauton, the cook, watching with malicious interest and delight the whole performance. "Now surely he will take him," we both exclaimed, as the deer in turning presented a full broad-side to our redoubtable champion of the target. But, *mirabile dictu*, he again missed him, and widely as ever, and on the heels of the report came booming over the waters Joe's loud, angry, "sacre, sacre."

Taylor, at this juncture, bethought him of the double-barreled breech-loader, charged with buckshot cartridge, which we had given him on leaving camp, enjoining him to be sure and use it if the rifle missed. But he had pooh-poohed our suggestions, saying that "he would rather depend on his old rifle than all the buckshot loaders that were ever made," and so he well might, for all the good that either of them did him.

His first shot was as futile as any of the others, and his second, which immediately followed, was very near being fatal to us instead of the deer. Though we were standing more than twenty feet above the level of the deer, yet the heavy shot came whizzing past our ears where we stood on the bank, and pattered down on the leaves and underbrush on every side of us. "Mon Dieu," yelled Tauton, "what's dat? The crazy fellah will kill us," and turning on his heel he bounded off through the woods as if a legion of devils were after him.

My loud shouts and gestures now drew the attention of the deer, as he rapidly neared the shore, and again turned him, as I intended, back into the lake, though towards a jutting point not far ahead of him. And now came the crowning act of silly conceit and dense stupidity. Instead of laying down his gun, as we heard Joe imploring him to do, and using the paddle, in order to force the deer into the middle of the lake, he must needs reload his gun and try his shooting again, but his hand was so shaky that he couldn't get the cartridge into place until it was too late, and though he got another shot, it was a miss like the rest, and the gallant buck, who had so nobly swam for his life, gained the shore, and was out of sight in a twinkling in the depths of the forest.

It was without doubt, the most blundering and disgraceful "let out" that I ever knew.

When Taylor made his appearance at the camp, old Tauton assailed him with the fiercest and most cutting maledictions. "Be gar, what you come up here for? Teach us how to shoot de deer. Be gar, me kill more deer with my old saucepan than you with de big rifle."

The poor man looked so humiliated, woe-begone, and utterly crest-fallen that I couldn't find it in my heart to say a word to him. But Tauton's wrath and tongue would not be appeased until, finally, Taylor seized his rifle, and swearing he would not return till he shot the deer and brought it back with him to the camp, started off into the woods. And as we saw neither him nor the deer again, I suppose he had been as unsuccessful on the land as he had been on the water.

CHAPTER XVI.

A Providential Dream.

TO me there has always appeared an inexplicable mystery enveloping the whole question of dreams. I believe it is yet a *terra incognita* to the psychologist and metaphysician, a vast, unexplored land—like the Antartic world with its lofty precipitous barriers of ice, which no man has yet been able to scale—baffling the most persevering and ingenious mental investigators. The only insight we have gained into this mysterious unknown region has been as misty, undefined, and tantalizing as that revealed by the smoke and fire vomited forth from the distant peaks of volcanoes, seen over the icy walls which encircle, and insurmountably hem in this Southern Polar world. To my mind, dreamland borders very closely upon the supernatural, and is one of the strongest collateral evidences against positivism in any shape or form. However, without going any further in this direction at present, let me tell my story of a remarkable dream that I once had, whereby I firmly believe my life was saved. I will narrate the dream with all its postcedent occurrences, in a plain, simple, unexaggerated way, without qualifying or distorting a single fact or detail; and in the same connection I will describe another dream, narrated to me, I believe, in the same tone and spirit of matter-of-fact circumstantiality, by the party himself, viz.: Duncan, the manager. And then, reader, you can draw your own conclusions and theories on the question, and if you and I are of the same mind at the end of the chapter, then I shall be glad—if not, we must agree to differ.

One morning I agreed to watch a certain headland on Long Lake, where we were hunting deer at the time. I had never been at the spot before, and was directed to it by Joe Le—, who was the "master of our hounds" and general director of our sports on that hunt. As I approached the point, I became conscious of a strange kind of acquaintanceship with the place. I knew positively that I had never been in that locality in my life, and yet the nearer I approached, and the closer I looked, a more positive remembrance of it arose, which I could not define, or locate in my mind.

Having beached my canoe, I looked about for a comfortable seat from which I could have a good out-look over the lake and adjoining shore. This I soon found in a snug niche in a mossy rock, which had been formed by the frost cracking out a triangular piece of the stone, making a seat as easy as an arm-chair. Even this peculiar feature of the place seemed singularly familiar to me. However, I was soon seated, and on the *qui-vive* for any sounds of deer and dogs. As I reclined luxuriously in my mossy nook I began to wonder why the place seemed so familiar to me, and looked around to see if I could find any further points of remembrance. My eye at once lit upon a tall, scraggy pine growing a short distance behind me, and lodged among its upper limbs was a larger branch, or rather trunk, of the top portion of another tree with its smaller dead branches attached, which had been blown there by some violent gust of wind, and not, as it seemed to me, very securely lodged either. The moment my eye fell on the tree a quick flash of vivid remembrance of having seen it before came into my mind, though when or how I could not tell. As I curiously gazed at the tree the idea arose, and gradually grew upon me, suppose that large branch were to become dislodged, it would in all probability fall right on the spot where I am sitting. Do as I liked I couldn't get this idea out of my mind, and it so impressed and awed me that, almost involuntarily, I arose and left the place.

Altogether I felt so uneasy, not exactly alarmed, that I re-entered my canoe, and paddled some three or four acres higher up the lake to another point of observation.

After a lapse of two or three hours I heard the signal from a distant part of the lake that the chase was over.

As I repassed the spot where I first intended to watch, I saw, to my utter amazement, and with no small degree of awe and thanksgiving, that the ominous-looking branch had fallen from the top of the pine directly upon the seat which I had vacated two hours before. Hastily landing, I closely examined the place; and the more I looked at it, the more I was convinced that if I had remained there, I would certainly have been crushed to death. The branch, or trunk, was more than a foot in diameter, and had attached to it a perfect network of dry, jagged limbs, and had so fallen that even though I had been watching it, I could hardly have had time to escape; and what made it still more remarkable was the fact that scarcely a breath of wind was stirring at the time.

As I stood rooted to the spot, and reflecting with profound gratitude and awe upon my narrow escape from a terrible death, the whole mystery of my strange acquaintance with the place suddenly cleared up. *I had dreamed it all the night before!* As clear as sunshine, I remembered now how in the unconscious mood of deep overpowering sleep, in the earlier hours of the night, I had pre-enacted the whole scenes and occurrences of the morning. Every detail of the dream recurred to me now, mirrored in the shore, the triangular seat, the tall pine with its scraggy top appendage, and its falling upon the seat I was occupying, though with the return of bright sunny day-light, and in the overflowing careless exuberance of health and high animal spirits, it had passed entirely from my mind for the time.

It had proved to me, however, as providential a dream as ever came to man in the balmy hours of slumber. For I felt convinced at the time, and am to this day, that, judging from the ordinary probabilities of the position, and the usual feelings and habits which regulate a person's actions in such circumstances, I should never have thought of leaving the point of observation, or even changing my seat, unless I had been influenced and impelled by that strange feeling of familiarity and remembrance,

M

which kept working and fermenting within me, and, unconsciously to myself, warned and admonished me.

Wise, thoughtful, **metaphysical,** clear-thinking, mystery-solving, dream-learned reader, what do think of this, *my* dream ?

Let me now tell you Duncan's dream, or rather the one in which he was the principal actor, which in many points of view is still more inexplicable, at least in the ordinarily accepted, and would-be thought learned, interpretation of dreams.

In a subsequent chapter I will speak about "jams," their existing perils, their hair-breadth escapes, and all their adventurous and hazardous interest. One of these of more than ordinary magnitude and difficulty occurred in the rapids at Carlton Place, on a "drive" in which Duncan was one of the foremen.

The rapids at that time were very different from what they are now. There were none of the side-dams, and other improvements which now makes their passage comparatively easy. At that time they were in their natural state, and were exceedingly difficult and dangerous to "drive."

On the occasion we speak of three or four concerns had got all mixed up together on the river, forming one conjunct drive of about fourteen thousand pieces of timber, and manned by over five hundred hands.

It was of course a busy time with them all, and many a tough and exciting piece of work they had together, at the various points of difficulty on the river. But this "jam" was a "terror" of a jam. It occurred at the most dangerous spot in the rapids, where the water was divided into two channels by an island, and descended on both sides with race-horse speed in a succession of small, tumbling, foaming cataracts.

The timber here got jammed together for half a mile up the river, and lay many tiers deep. Thousands of sticks were inextricably mixed up together, and much of it stood on end, out of the foaming waters. It was an awful scene of piled-up confusion. If you were to take an armful of straw and throw it into a boiling cauldron it would, ten minutes after, give you some idea of the spectacle that jam presented.

For three days the combined crews had been prying, and pinching, and tugging at the key sticks, and other knotty joints of the mass, but in vain. The "jam" defied their utmost efforts and ingenuity, and remained as firmly locked as ever.

On the evening of the third day a council of all the foremen was called, and it was decided that the next day one man should assume full control, and direct the whole combined movement, and Duncan, on account of his experience and ability, was unanimously chosen.

The next morning as he was proceeding to the scene of operations, his companion, who was a particular friend of his, told him that he had had a remarkable dream the night before, which so impressed him that he felt he must tell it to him, even at the risk of being laughed at, which Duncan said he might have done if it had been any one else than Fred R—; but Fred was a grave, steady-going, no-nonsense sort of a man, and an old experienced and fearless river driver—the last man in the world, in fact, who would be needlessly or sentimentally affected by a dream or anything else.

The dream was this—Duncan and he had worked together, shoulder by shoulder, the whole day, and towards evening, after every man had been sent safely ashore, and they were about to give the last pry to the "jam," it suddenly burst, and in a moment the whole mass was in a whirl and jumble of violent commotion, and their retreat to the shore was cut off. At this crisis of life or death Fred saw a large black charred log suddenly shoot out from the boiling, seething mass, and float clear ahead into the rapids below, and before he knew how, both he and Duncan found themselves safely standing upon it, and riding clear and securely in advance of the whirling, tossing timbers through the foaming swells into the calm waters below.

He narrated the dream with such circumstantiality of detail, and in such a serious manner, that Duncan was greatly impressed, and especially when Fred told him that he had dreamed it twice over, and each time with precisely the same particulars.

"Fred," said he, "if it comes to the worst, we will look out for the old black stick."

Sure enough this most remarkable dream came true in every and the minutest particulars.

When the critical moment came, and, as is customary in such cases, every man was sent ashore, and he and Fred were about to give the last heave, the jam did burst before they were fully prepared, and in a moment they were both in the very jaws of death. Duncan, in his grave, solemn manner, told me that he never in his life witnessed such a scene of awful and wild confusion. The heaviest timbers were broken and twisted like withes, some of them were heaved bodily into the air, and as the pent-up mass, and dammed-up waters broke away they tore up the banks on either side, uprooted the tallest trees and the heaviest rocks, and carried them bodily with them into the boiling, seething, thundering current. He thought it was all over with them, when suddenly the black charred log of Fred's dream shot past them, and almost involuntarily, and unknowingly, they leaped upon it and rode out from the rest of the timber, and passed with the speed of lightning through the foaming rapids into the calm waters below.

This is the dream, with all its accompaniments, exactly as Duncan told it to me, and, so far from having any reason to doubt its veracity, or even any exaggeration or distortion in its account, I give it my fullest and most implicit credence. Certainly, equally with my own, it was a providential dream for Duncan and Fred.

I am no hand at moralizing, nor of probing deeply into the causes and secret springs of things. I like to deal with facts, actions and effects—there are quite enough of these cropping up in the ordinary walks of life to enable a man to shape his own course, and to formulate opinion both as to himself and others, and their common environments. Now as to the foregoing dreams and all of a like character—and who is there that has not had them I hold that they not only demonstrate the actuality of the supernatural, but also teach plainly that it comes nearer to us in this present life, yea, touches us more closely than we at all realize. Who can tell but that it is with us in every onward step of the journey—is interwoven with the variegated web of our mortal life, enters into and permeates as a subtle essence the great actions, events and movements of our lives. God is nearer to us—near in the sense of a great actual, tangible, positive fact—than we suppose. And it is this grand, sublime fact that men of shallow thought, of superficial reflection, of negative faith, whose mental and moral horizon is bounded by their earthly vision, and whose desires, aspirations, and ambitions are all centred in this present state of things, cannot recognize, understand, or realize.

"For God speaketh once, yea twice, yet man perceiveth it not.

"In a dream, in a vision of the night, when deep sleep falleth upon men, in slumberings upon the bed;

"Then he openeth the ears of men, and sealeth their instruction,

"That he may withdraw man from his purpose, and hide pride from man.

"He keepeth back his soul from the pit, and his life from perishing by the sword."

Job xxxiii. 14-18.

CHAPTER XVII.

" Did you ever know what it is to be blind ? I have !"

I have a great dread of fire-arms, I mean of their careless handling in the woods, or, in fact, anywhere. No man can be too careful how he handles his gun or revolver. Nine-tenths of the casualties that occur are the result, not of mere accident, or unforeseen, unaccountable, and, humanly speaking, unpreventable causes, but of gross, rank, inexcusable mismanagement. And, considering how frequently people misbehave in this direction, the wonder is that there are not a great many more accidents than there are. If I were an autocrat I would put in the pillory every man who was convicted of a careless, trifling handling of any fire-arm. A summary and severe punishing of these offenders would soon teach them common-sense and ordinary propriety in this most flagrant and unpardonable foolery.

But it is not mere carelessness that oftentimes causes these appalling accidents to life and limb, of which we constantly read and hear, but *deliberate* fooling, and " larking " with fire-arms, such as pointing the muzzle at a person, snapping the cap, and silly jokes of this kind. Every person who thus uses even an empty gun should be publicly whipped. I have been dreadfully provoked with fools of this stamp, and have neither patience nor leniency in speaking and dealing with them. Any sorrow or remorse that they may feel in consequence of accidents they may cause, I would regard with as little consideration as I would the maudliness of an old toper who waters his whiskey with his tears.

I remember once on Paul's lake when, after supper, we were all standing around the camp fire, a silly, scatter-brain fellow who prided himself upon playing practical jokes, in order to give us a start, threw a rifle cartridge into the fire; it caused of course a great explosion and scattering of the fire and ashes but was within a hair's-breadth of causing the death of Mr. B. C——, an influential and wealthy lumber merchant, who was our guest at the time. The ball whizzed past his ear, almost grazing it, a half inch nearer and it would have killed him on the spot. Mr. C—— was so annoyed and disgusted that he left us the next morning. If we had served that fellow right we should have ducked him in the lake, and sent him home to his mother.

I have seen so many narrow escapes and some few accidents that I made it a rule to myself never, under any circumstances whatsoever, to have the muzzle of my gun pointed at a person or even in his direction. If I am walking in the woods *behind* a companion I carry my gun on my shoulder, with the muzzle pointing backwards; if *before* him, in the hollow of my arm, pointing ahead. This rule, from strict observance, has become a *habit* with me, so that, even unconsciously, I observe it. On one occasion this habit was the means of saving my old and faithful friend Tauton from a terrible, perhaps fatal, accident. As we were tramping through the bush we were threatened with a shower of rain, and I thought it advisable to put my fowling-piece into the heavy leathern case which Tauton was carrying; so, seating himself on a log, he held the lower end of the case while I inserted the gun into the other end. While doing this I noticed that the muzzle pointed towards his thigh, almost mechanically I turned it a little aside. I had hardly done so when, in some unaccountable way which I could never understand, the gun went off, tearing the case to slivers. "Mon Dieu, mon Dieu, I'm shot,

I'm shot," yelled the old man, in most heart-rending accents, clasping, as he spoke, his thigh, with both hands. If ever there was a terror-stricken individual in this world I was that person. From Tauton's ghastly looks and agonizing howls I felt sure the whole charge had gone into him. Such, however, by this providential movement of mine, was not the case; but one of the slivers of the thick leather case, by the force of the explosion, came down upon his immense fat thigh with such a thwack as to cause him as much pain for the time as if he had been shot. Never did school-boy get a more stinging " lick " from an irate dominie than did Tauton from that thick jagged strap. No wonder he howled with pain; and felt " sure " he was done for, and never were men more devoutly thankful than we when we discovered the real extent of his injury. But his thigh was black and blue for a week afterwards, and he carried the mark of that " lick " for many a month. It was, however, a close escape; if the gun had gone off a second or two sooner his thigh would have been shattered, and in the position we were at the time he would in all probability have perished before I could have brought him assistance.

The introduction of breech-loaders has tended greatly to lessen the number of gun accidents; but even yet they are frequent enough in their occurrence, and this even with the safest and most approved mechanical construction. I met with an accident at one time with my Ballard rifle, one of the safest, most convenient, and accurate shooting-pieces that a man can take to the backwoods. It was a serious enough affair at the time, and would have been much more so if it had not been for the prompt kindness of my companion, Aleck Y——and the skillful surgery of my old friend, Dr. F——. It is the occasion of the peculiar query and answer which form the title of this chapter.

My month's leave of absence was just out; I had spent it mainly in Aleck's shanty, and spun it out, as I always did, to the uttermost limit. As Aleck and I were on our way to the settlements we stopped on a bridge over the Clide to shoot at an object lying about a hundred yards up the river on the ice. It was a capital target at which to test the merits of our respective rifles, concerning which we were always at variance. As I reloaded in a great hurry, I did not thrust the cartridge sufficiently home into the breech—the barrel was somewhat dirty, and the cartridge slightly rusty and difficult to shove in tight and close; not noticing this in my hurry, I drew the block up with the usual jerk, raising the rifle at the same time to take aim. The consequence was that the upper part of the block struck the lower portion of the slightly protruding cartridge and exploded it before the block had reached its proper place behind the cartridge. The result was the whole charge of powder, with the bottom fragments of the cartridge, went right into my face at not more than a foot's distance from it. I was thrown several feet and knocked insensible. When I recovered my senses, I found myself on my knees, rubbing the snow with both hands into my burning eyes. The pain was excruciating, and I believe it was the instantaneous, unwitting application of the cold snow which tended to neutralize the dangerous effect of the fiery sheet of flame which flashed into my eyes, and saved me from an immediate and permanent blindness. In this opinion I am confirmed by several physicians with whom I have conversed on the matter since. However, for the time being, everything was dark and horrible about me, and I felt, rather than thought, that I was blind—blinded for life. Oh, the horror of that thought which grew upon me as I became more and more conscious. In the meantime Aleck had hoisted me on to his broad shoulders, and was carrying me with what speed he could to the nearest house, which was about a mile distant. It was well for him and me that he was one of the Goliaths of the forest, a man of herculean strength. As he told me afterwards, he hardly knew what he was doing. He was almost as much stunned as I was, for he thought at first I was killed and when the blood streamed from my face, when I became sensible, he felt sure I was badly injured. It took him about an hour to get me to the house, and such an hour of unutterable misery I never passed in my life. The pain in my eyes and face was utterly forgotten in the terrible, absorbing thought that I had lost my eyesight. Everything was black as midnight around me. My eyes seemed hermetically sealed, and I felt paralysed with an awful sense of helplessness and hopelessness. But my inner perceptions were keenly and sensitively alive. Visions of men who had had their eyes blown out by blasts, of distorted, blue-stained, sightless faces, of groping, weary-looking, staff-leaning men, and of long months and years of coming darkness and loneliness came floating through my mind, with a horribly realistic distinctness. Reader, I hope you may never know what it is to be blind, either in reality or imagination.

On our arrival at the house, the proprietor of which, Adam C——, was a lifelong and staunch friend of mine, I received every attention which unbounded kindness and **hospitality could bestow**. His wife bathed my face **and head** copiously with cool, soothing lotions, **and** gradually I became able to open my eyelids and bear the light, and after a while was able to see dimly about me. Oh, the unexpressible relief and delight at finding that I had still a certain **use of my eyes, and** how quickly, in the revulsion of feeling, I became sanguine and comparatively cheerful. In a short time they had rigged up a kind of jumper, and **Aleck and I were** once more *en route* for the nearest **doctor's place, which** was at Lanark, twelve miles **distant**.

That night Dr. F—— cut out more than a hundred **grains of** powder that had been buried deep in my face by **the force of** the explosion, and a piece of cartridge a half-inch in length out of my right eye. I was laid up for a week in a darkened room, and then pronounced convalescent, and fit to travel.

I cannot too strongly caution every sportsman who uses cartridges with a circular fire to be certain that the cartridge is pushed closely home, and plumb with the inner rim of the breech, before he pulls up the block to its proper position. Otherwise he will run the risk of having his eyes blown out as I did, or, at least of having his face badly disfigured, which I **also** happily escaped through the immediate and skilful **surgery of** Dr. F——. *Verbum sapientis* sat.

CHAPTER XVIII.

A Night on the Lake in a Snow-storm.

ONE of the most perilous and terrible experiences a man can pass through is to be caught in a snow-storm on one of our broad backwoods lakes. These storms then assume the form of what are called in our North-west prairies "blizzards," and can be braved with impunity by neither man nor beast.

One can have no conception of their wild, furious nature until he has witnessed them. It is a blinding chaos of whirling snow. Owing to the peculiar surroundings of some of these lakes—generally high precipitous banks fissured by wide, deep gullies—the wind comes sweeping down in howling, isolated tornadoes. These meet and intersect each other with terrific violence, and produce a most appalling effect. The stoutest heart will soon quail, and the sturdiest frame succumb before their power. In such circumstances it is most dangerous to go more than a few yards from the shore, for the moment you lose sight of it your course is all hap-hazard, and, becoming bewildered, you flounder about at the mercy of the tempest.

A most dreadful casualty occurred during the prevalence of one of these storms, while I was in the backwoods. Two men, on their way to one of the shanties, attempted to cross a lake some miles in width. It was an act of madness. Better far to have gone round the lake and risked the dangers of falling trees and flying limbs than attempted this. The poor fellows soon became bewildered by the whirling drift and piercing blasts, which seemed to come from all points of the compass at once. Finally one of them, overcome by the cold and fatigue, lay down in the snow, and, notwithstanding the entreaties and exertions of his companion, refused to make any further effort, and was left to perish miserably and alone in the storm. The other man, after some hours of incredible exertion, arrived at the shanty, but in such an exhausted and frost-bitten condition that he died in terrible agony a few hours after his arrival.

Another incident, under somewhat similar circumstances, though happily with a different ending, occurred some time previous to this, not half a mile from the shanty where I was staying. A well-known Presbyterian minister, while on a missionary tour through the district, got caught in one of these storms. He was driving his own horse and cutter, and had his son with him, a boy of about ten years.

As he neared the shanty, some time after dark, he had occasion to cross a small lake, not more than a quarter of a mile wide, where the road ran. He had no sooner emerged from the forest, and was fairly out on the lake than the full force of the storm burst upon him, and such was its blinding fury that he soon became completely bewildered. His horse left the road, and floundered here and there in vain attempts to recover it. He was placed, indeed, in a terrible position. In the darkness of the night and the howling swirl of the cutting drift nothing can possibly be conceived more appalling. If his perilous position had only been known at the shanty how quickly would a score of brave hearts and stalwarth frames been out for his succor.

He was not a man, however, to give up in despair. After many fruitless attempts to recover the road, and not knowing where he might wander to, he resolved to make the best of his position, and wait where he was till daylight.

He had two buffalo robes in the cutter, and the horse cover. His first care was for his little boy. Wrapping him carefully up in both robes, he placed him at the bottom of the cutter; then strapping the cover tightly round his faithful horse, he bethought of himself. His only safety was in active and continuous exertion. So drawing his sash more tightly round his heavy fur coat, he walked round and round his precious charge the whole night.

What a long, weary vigil it must have been! How the leaden-winged hours must slowly have flown past, through the dreary darkness, and cold, and storm. For twelve hours, which must have seemed a life-time to him, he kept up his continuous tramp, tramp, varied only by a hasty, sudden run as he felt the piercing cold about to overcome him. Many a wistful look he would cast about him to catch the first token of the long coming daylight, and many a time his stout heart must have felt ready to succumb before that terrible ordeal of fatigue, cold and drowsiness.

At length day broke, the road was regained, and the shanty reached just about sunrise.

Strange to say, neither he nor his little son were any the worse of their fearful night's experience. The foreman, who told me the story, and whom I heard frequently refer to it since, could never do so without great emotion.

CHAPTER XIX.

About Mines, etc.

IT would be much more easy to write a readable than a reliable chapter on this subject. For here, as elsewhere throughout the world, mining questions are invested with all sorts of imaginary possibilities, varying in every degree of magnitude according to the hopes and speculations of the intertested parties. At present, and for some time back, there is considerable excitement over the mineral question in this section, consequently it is almost impossible to obtain determinate data on which to base an honest and sound opinion. However, this much we can affirm, that it is the full belief of many most intelligent and prominent individuals, both here and elsewhere, that this country, poor and worthless in an agricultural point of view, and being rapidly denuded of its timber products, is a vast reservoir of incalculable mineral wealth.

Indications of almost every economic mineral, except coal, have been found, and scientific experts have declared that many of those are of the purest quality, and found also in geological surroundings and connections that seem to justify the expectation that, if developed, they would yield, in most cases paying, in some inexhaustible, quantities. Notwithstanding those favorable auguries, there is no undue excitement, or anything approaching a mining fever among the people. There is too much of the Scotch element among them, with its characteristic coolness and caution, for this. You can easily see, however, that each settler is a prospector on his own land, and if he discovers, or thinks he does, any mineral indications on it, he is quite sufficiently alive to its value and importance. It is a great mistake to suppose that you can drive an easy one-sided bargain with these unsophisticated backwoodsmen.

I have been greatly amused at some fellows "from town"—sharp, long-headed, knowing chaps, thoroughly "up on 'Change," and posted in all the tricks of "bulling," "bearing" and "cornering"— who have come out to these regions, and, in the plenitude of their superior knowledge and astuteness, thought they could have it all their own way with the simple-minded habitants. It is intensely edifying to an onlooker who knows pretty well the character of both parties to watch the process of bargaining between the two. The cunning side wink of the town man, as much as to say, "I'll show you how to manage this fellow," his indifferent handling of a great roll of one-dollar bank-notes, his wise, knowing talk about quartz, horn-blende, strata, veins, pockets, the latest quotations of the mineral market, and all the other jargon of the mining stock-broker, wherewith he supposes he is mystifying and circumventing the innocent rustic; but he little knows all the time how this supposed simpleton is "fulling him to the top of his bent," and playing his own little game with him. If the "sharp un" thinks he can find out the exact *locale* of the mine in question, or obtain from the settler a deed in full of all mineral rights on his sterile, rocky, fireswept lot for a mere nominal sum, he makes a woeful mistake. You need to get up a little earlier in the morning than you are accustomed to if you expect to get the better of these quiet, slow-tongued, witless-looking backwoodsmen.

A very common mode of attempted outwitting of each other between these two parties is for the speculator to engage the backwoodsman to go with him on a prospecting through the country. By offering him three dollars or more a day, and good living besides, he thinks to secure his services in finding out the spots where the ore is, and then, if it be not already deeded property, he can easily secure it, if he thinks it is worth his while. But the backwoodsman has no such intention as this in his mind. He is quite willing to take all the pay he can possibly get, and give him all the prospecting and tramping he can desire, and for as long a time as possible, but he takes very good care to keep clear of the spot where he knows the mineral is. Oh, no, he will not divulge that all-important secret, not for all the blandishments and cajoleries that can be lavished on him. He will lead his victim for weeks through the woods and among the hills, but he will not impart to him any really valuable discovery unless for a plump, round sum in hard cash, or for a profitable share in any after-working of the mine.

There is nothing in which town and city people make a greater mistake than in their under-estimation of the character and mental ability of the dwellers in the backwoods. No doubt the latter are not so quick in their perceptions and advanced in their ideas as the former, and their thoughts and mental activities are confined to a comparatively narrow area; but within that area they are much more thoughtful, have much shrewder conceptions and sounder judgments than their countrymen of town or city life, in their enlarged, almost world-wide, sphere.

The great mass of those who live in the cities have such a variety of subjects to engage their attention—in fact a continuous panorama of new and sensational objects is always passing before their eyes—not only in their immediate surroundings, but from every part of the globe—that a superficialty of thought is engendered,—their mental and reasoning processes are mere skimming operations, and hence their judgments and determinations are necessarily often weak, shallow and worthless. There is too much newspaper reading now-a-days, in fact, it is the sole literature of great masses of our middle and upper classes; eight-sheeted daily papers at a cent a copy, containing every possible variety of matter, from the trimmings of my lady's satin dress at last night's ball up to the overturnings of governments and nations, are spread out night after night before the artizan, merchant and professional man; and this variety and multiplicity of subjects so engross their attention that they have no time for solid thought or reflection, and such a process as mental digestion, even of what they do read is utterly unknown to them. The consequence must necessarily be what we have said, flippancy, shallowness, hasty and unreliable judgments.

But the backwoodsman's habitude of life moulds

his attitude of mind. He reads and speaks little, but thinks a great deal. Within the narrow sphere in which he moves he has great concentration of thought, and sober and solid reflection. Consequently, **his** determinations are generally sound and correct. His local weekly gives him all the information **he** wants about the outer world. After that he is like the wise man we have heard of, who made five hundred pounds a year by simply minding his own business.

However, to get back to the point in question: **if a man who** is tolerably well up in mineral matters goes out **to this** country with some money **in** his pocket, **and is** prepared to deal fairly and in a straightforward manner with the people, he will find abundant opportunities for most profitable investments, either in buying the mineral rights on deeded lands, or obtaining patents **for** wild lands.

Fair specime**ns of gold have** been found, also of silver; **copper in some** localities is in abundance, specimens of **the best** quality of mica, as large as **twelve** by fourteen inches, have been taken out just at the surface; molybdenum of the purest quality and **in great** abundance has been **discovered,** graphite also, **and indi**cations of phosphate, **though not** yet of a very pronounced character, have been disclosed; lead in some places is in inexhaustible quantities. But the mineral which, above all others, abounds and characterises the country is iron. If there is "anything in iron," here, emphatically, is the country for it. There is no better in the world. Though it is yet only in the embryo state of development still large investments have been made, and deep shafts have sunk, and mining in the technical sense of the term is now carried on by six wealthy and influential companies and with most profitable results. These companies are: the Robertsville, sixty miles north of Kingston; the Bethlehem Company of Pennsylvania and the Boyd Caldwell just alongside (the Bethlehem is on lease from Caldwell, the owner, at a very fair royalty), nine miles further on; the Caldwell (W. C.) & Gildersleeve, thirteen miles further north; the Sherrit & Radenhurst, half a mile distant; and the Elliot, Thompson & Johnston mine, on Calabogie lake, twelve miles further north. All these mines are situated directly on the line of the Kingston and Pembroke Railway, or so close to it that the longest switch is not more than half a mile. Thus the ore is dumped directly from the pit into the car, obviating all need of cartage.

Comparisons are always difficult, and ugly things to deal in, and it is quite sufficient for our purpose to say that each proprietor is quite satisfied with his own mine both as to quantity of the yield, and quality of the ore, and is fully confident that there is a fortune in his holding.

The output of ore from these mines is entirely from magnetic veins, with a percentage of about 60 of metallic iron. Hematite is found in deposits, but this is not so profitable for permanent working as the former. Large veins, as well as deposits, of the richest hematite are found in the adjoining townships of Dalhousie and Lanark, but these are yet undeveloped—a ripe and rich harvest for capital and enterprise.

The iron market, notwithstanding the heavy and ponderous nature of the article itself, is the most capricious and uncertain in the world. It is fickle and variable as a woman's temper, it goes up and down from the most trivial causes, and sometimes apparently from no cause at all. At this present time it is depressed to a lower point than at any period since 1879, but next month it may be up again to par, and perhaps many degrees above it. Consequently the output of ore, as well as the opening up and developing of new mines by fresh capitalists, is largely affected by this irregularity of the market, and hence, as we remarked at the opening of this chapter, it is very difficult to give a reliable and determinate judgment on this question, otherwise than in this general way, "the iron is *there*, in inexhaustible quantity and the purest quality."

But, as we have seen, that great civilizer and developer of natural products, the "iron-horse," has come, and is rushing and shrieking through the land, and every possible interest of every dweller in this section, from the humblest laborer to the wealthiest capitalist, and from hop-poles up to gold diggings, has received thereby a mighty impulse and onward impetus. The K. & P. R. is one of the boldest, and most enterprising, and, as it is now proving to be, one of the most successful undertakings, of the present day in Canada. Five years ago not one in a thousand who was acquainted with that country of giant rocky hills, of vast jungles, of deep boggy morasses, of lakes, rivers and forest, had any faith in its practicability; but the far-seeing, intelligent resolution and capital of those enterprising Americans, the Folger Bros., of Kingston, have made an accomplished fact of what was deemed an absolute impossibility. This whole section of country owes a debt of obligation to these men which it can never sufficiently acknowledge or requite. The elder brother who is familiarly, but never disrespectfully, called

Ben, **and** whose portrait will at once be recognised, is the very embodiment of push and energy, as well as of liberal and generous action. I have been told by gentlemen who have had frequent dealings with him that "he can talk as much business in **ten** minutes as most men can do in an hour,"—an invaluable quality in business affairs. The magnitude of the work which they undertook, and have accomplished so far, over the most difficult section of the route, will at once be understood when I state that no less than eight firms of contractors have engaged **for** the construction of the road, but one after another has withdrawn or failed, owing to the immense expense and difficulty of the undertaking.

The present contractors, however, viz.: Messrs. Chisholm, McDonald & O'Brien, are men of the right calibre, and have just undertaken a fresh contract for the completion of the whole line to Renfrew. Mr. M. J. O'Brien, who superintends the practical work of the road, though a comparatively young man, not yet thirty, has already gained a high reputation in the Dominion as an energetic, talented railroad man. He and his *confrères* possess the full confidence of the Company in their ability to carry on the work to a speedy and successful accomplishment.

Enterprise and Capital (New School).

A few facts here as to some of the difficulties that have to be overcome in building this road may not be uninteresting even to the general reader. At Bluff Point, which is a rocky promontory at the foot of Calabogie lake, there is a cutting through the solid rock from which 24,000 cubic yards of rock have to be taken, the largest rock cutting in Canada, except the Morissy rock cutting in the Intercolonial. The approach to this promontory is through the lake across the mouth of Grassy Bay, a distance of 3,000 feet, and it will take 40,000 yards of solid rock to "fill up" this water gap; this one mile of the line costing over $70,000. At another spot, called Mud lake, though it is not larger than an ordinary mill pond, being only 650 feet wide, it has taken 23,000 cubic yards of rock, and innumerable tons of gravel and earth to "fill up" a line directly across, as, on account of the surroundings, it was found impossible to go round it. This aggravating, tantalizing bit of water, where a large force has been at work for over fifteen months, has been aptly re-christened by the contractors Deception Lake. It is to be hoped that the first heavy train that goes over it may not sink through, and be engulfed in the measureless depths of its muddy bottom. At another rock cutting, near Folger Station, seventy-four miles north of Kingston, and which took over six months to complete, there is a curiosity in the line of blasting skill lying within a few yards of the track—it is an immense rectangular block of solid rock, which weighs over seventy tons, and which was thrown several hundred feet, obliquely up the side of a hill; it is an object well worthy the notice of the passing traveller. The power of some of these blasts will be understood when I say that sometimes as much as 500 pounds of powder are used in one " shot," and at one blast in particular 136 cubic yards of rock were thrown out.

The whole road when graded and completed to Renfrew, on the Canada Pacific, a distance of 112 miles, is estimated to cost on an average $20,000 a mile, and the thorough equipment of it will cost $10,000 more. But, best of all, notwithstanding the immense difficulties and expense of the work, the road pays, and according to all human calculation will continue to do so, and that much more largely in the near future. The export freight of square timber, sawn lumber and iron ore is even now enormous, but nothing to what it will be as new mills are built, and fresh mines opened.

But this is not all—a glance at the map will at once show that this road, connecting with the

Canadian Pacific at Renfrew, will be the shortest and most direct route, via Kingston, to Oswego, New York and all points West. Then it will not only be the great highway for all lumbering supplies, pork, flour, etc., from Chicago and the West, for Central Ontario and the Upper Ottawa, but also for travel and traffic, during the open months of the year at least, from Manitoba and the North-west to these great emporiums of trade and commerce, both in the east and west of the United States.

In conclusion, I feel assured in saying, and in this I am confirmed by those who are thoroughly posted in these matters, that the Kingston and Pembroke Railway, when fully equipped and in running order, will be one of the best-paying enterprises in the Dominion of Canada.

This whole section of country, therefore, through the building and working of the railway, will yet, and very shortly, become one of the richest heritages with which bountiful nature has blessed us, that is, provided proper precautions are taken as to forest fires and the preservation of our standing and fallen timber, the development of our mineral resources, according to their natural capabilities, and the preventing of settlers coming into the country as agricultural workers.

o

CHAPTER XX.

Lost in the Woods.

THE sensation of being lost in the woods is one of the most frightful that can afflict a sentient human being. It is a species of mental aberration, or rather of incipient madness, in which you have the consciousness, in its fullest torture, of being out of your head, and, if possible, of getting worse and worse all the time. It is not, therefore, simply getting astray in the bush, and knowing it, and just wandering on, trusting to chance to hit on the right track, or get out somehow,—this is a common occurrence with backwoodsmen, and, apart from its inconvenience, exposure and fatigue, occasions them very little uneasiness. No, the lost in the woods to which I refer is a very different thing indeed. It is a mental affection, a perfect loss of self-possession, and an utter abandonment to any fancy, whim, or hallucination that may float into the mind; and the result of it is an aimless, frantic, feverish wandering, and hurrying through the bush, until finally, from absolute exhaustion, the poor wretch will sink down and die from hunger and exposure. In such a case there is no hope of the "lost one," unless he is found by searching parties, or stumbles, by the merest chance, on a clearing or some bushranger. His own sense and reason will never in the world extricate him. I cannot illustrate this better than by an incident in point which was related to me by Duncan, the manager.

The lost party in this case was Tom, the cook, who one day took it in his head to go by a short cut through the woods to visit a neighboring shanty. This cut was about three miles in length, but would save him a round of seven miles by the regular road.

Duncan and some of his men had frequently gone by the short road, but it was dangerous for any one except an experienced bushman, for it was not even, "blazed out," and led through thick swamps, and round small lakes. The cook, though he had never been through by that route, and was, besides, rather a green hand in the bush, resolved to attempt it, and the result was he got lost, fairly lost, in the sense I speak of.

Not returning to his own shanty by nightfall, as was expected, Duncan crossed over by first daylight, and found he had not arrived at the other shanty the day before. So, knowing the nature of the bush and the inexperience of the man, he set out to look for him. In company with Ned R—— one of the foremen, he ranged the woods the whole day in every direction between the two shanties, but found no trace of Tom, so the next day the whole combined force of the two shanties, "all hands and the cook," as they say, turned out to search the woods. Still no trace of the poor fellow could be found.

The next day the search was continued; and late in the afternoon Duncan, in company with John C——, one of the most experienced and sagacious bushmen that ever ranged these woods, when crossing Redhorse lake in an old canoe which they found on the shore, saw the man standing on the bank they were approaching; he stood on a high rock like a monument, gazing abstractedly and sadly out on the lake in the very direction they were approaching; and though they yelled and whooped, and hurrahed in their delight at finding him, yet he never saw nor heard them, and as they landed just a few yards below him, he slowly and wearily turned his back on them, and walked into the bush. When they overtook him, which they very quickly did, he showed neither surprise nor joy, but seemed dazed and stupid.

The most remarkable thing in the whole affair

was that he had three partridges in his hand when they found him, which he told them he had shot—for he had a gun and plenty of ammunition with him—just an hour after leaving the shanty. And when they asked him why he didn't cook them, for he had matches too, he said he never thought of it, and he had carried them the whole four days in his hand.

It was several days before the man recovered his proper senses, and when he did he narrated most distinctly the route he had traversed, and described places, well-known to them, which he had passed. He said that one evening as he sat at the foot of a tree a large buck came and stood quite near him rubbing its immense antlers against a tree, and yet it never entered his head to shoot it, and yet, on other occasions, the man was a keen sportsman.

From the haggard, worn-out appearance of the man they were fully of the opinion that he would very soon have lain down, and never got up again.

It was the last time that Tom ever attempted to take that or any other short cut through an unknown bush, without a companion.

I had a taste of this horrible experience myself at one time, and I certainly never want another: I was rambling through the woods one morning round Middle Branch Lake when I was led out of my bearings by a rabbit. This animal is a most tantalizing brute to follow in the woods. It will bound out of sight in a twinkling, and then stop to wait till you sight it again when, before you can take aim, it will be off like a flash, and perhaps repeat this operation half-a-dozen times before you can bag him.

This rabbit was a particularly provoking fellow, and led me a long and winding chase before I finally shot him. When I did, at last, I found that he had led me completely out of my reckoning in the dark, dense swamp. I had not the remotest idea where I was, nor what course to take in order to extricate myself; still I did my best, and wandered on for some time till the conviction settled upon me that I was lost. Then it was that this horrible feeling I have spoken of took possession of me. It is, I believe, the worst phase of panic that can seize a man. It is bewilderment, terror, amazement, light-headedness all combined. I felt sense, reason, courage, all forsaking me. It was only by a strong exertion of will-power that I was able to preserve my self-possession. I remember perfectly sitting down on a log and saying to myself: "now, old chap, this kind of thing won't do, if you give way to this feeling you are done for."

And I did conquer the feeling; and when I recovered my self-possession, and was able calmly to think over the matter, I laughed aloud at the absurd length to which my excited and alarmed imagination had carried me.

What had I, after all, really to fear? Even though I was lost for days, or even weeks, what of it? I had a double-barreled fowling-piece, plenty of ammunition, matches, my pipe, and a full pouch of tobacco. I couldn't starve; for wild beasts I didn't care a rush; I could camp at night in a way that would defy any weather; and out of the woods I certainly would get somehow and some time or other.

Still I used my best endeavors to extricate myself as speedily as possible, and tried to fix my mind on what I thought was the right direction, and stick to it in a straight line.

After all I walked the whole day, and towards night—not in a very pleasant frame of mind, I must confess—I was looking about for a place to camp and cook my rabbit, when suddenly the clear stentorian voice of old Tauton singing, fell on my delighted ears.

Never did music sound more sweetly to me in my life, and, with all my affection for the old man, I felt that I never loved him so much as I did then. I could have fallen on his neck and embraced him in the exuberance of my feelings.

I immediately discharged both barrels of my gun and bounded in the direction of the resounding " En roulant," and there, not a hundred yards from the spot where I was about to camp, was the lake, and sitting in his canoe, a few yards from the shore, was old Tauton. The old fellow had become alarmed at my protracted absence, and had gone on a scouting tour round the lake which was full of deep bays, and was singing in his loudest key on purpose to let me hear, if within reach,—the very best method of being heard at a distance, in the woods, that a person can adopt. Shouting and hallooing can no more rival it then a Jew's harp can a war trumpet.

At the spot where I came out on the lake we were about two miles from the camp, to which the old fellow paddled me in great glee, and where I was received with loud demonstrations of welcome by my companions, who had given me up, for the night at least.

I suppose everybody has heard of the singular fact that when a person gets lost in the bush he very generally travels in a circle, or at all events in some strangely circuitous route, which will bring him back to the spot from which he started, or within a very short distance of it; and, what is still more remarkable, the wanderer almost invariably takes the left hand course from his starting-point. The theory of this singular action of the will—or the legs—I have never yet heard satisfactorily explained, though many very plausible ones are advanced by "the know every-things" in these matters; but as to the actuality of the phenomenon there can be no question. I have upon more than one occasion, when I have been led astray in the bush, undergone this experience, and I could recount scores of instances told me by bush-rangers of the same thing happening to themselves.

It is most amusing to hear these old veterans of the backwoods describing their sensations when they have been thus "fooled," fairly bamboozled, in their own native, and most familiar, element. When, after tramping many weary miles through the bush, and all the time going on in the full assurance that they were in the right direction, and in a perfectly straight course, they would unexpectedly find themselves at the very point from which they had started several hours before, their feelings can be better imagined than described. It is astonishment, rage, mortification, bewilderment, all combined, and, as I have already shewn, if they were to lose their self-possession they would as quickly be "done for," and as fairly "lost" as any green-hand that ever entered a bush. But it is very difficult to get those old stagers off their balance. They know better than to lose their heads in such straits as these, and they very speedily become as cool and self-collected in these mazy depths of the forest, as if they stood by their own camboose fire. I have often asked these old experienced bushmen what plan they adopt when they find themselves in such a position as I have described, and the answer I have received has almost invariably been the same from all of them.

I remember once interrogating old Pete C—— on this matter, and receiving an answer which was as characteristic of the man as it was *apropos* to the subject.

Pete was one of the most original and eccentric characters that ever graced backwoods life in the Ottawa Valley. Though only of medium height he was a perfect Falstaff in lateral dimensions. And yet he was supple and strong as any man need be. He could trot along under his burden of eighteen stone as lightly as a girl of sixteen, and shoulder his barrel of pork as readily as a hotel runner could your carpet bag. Pete was "no slouch," I can assure you. Though he used a most unsanctified familiarity with certain unmentionable adjectives which came hurtling from his mouth like projectiles from a mortar, yet his general speech had a savor of gravity, precision, and profound sapience in it which was wondrously edifying. "When I get into such a fix in the bush," he said, "I sit down on the nearest log, light my pipe, and calmly smoke and think over the matter. I then cast the eye of scrutiny over every quarter of the heavens and the earth, and there I sit, and will sit, until I know where I am, and in what direction I am to go, or I'll be d——d, frozen, or starved."

One of the best stories in this connection that I ever heard was about a Frenchman of the name of Paquette. One morning, about day-break, he started to go to another shanty, about twelve miles distant, situated on Upper Trout Lake. On leaving, the cook advised him to take a "snack" with him, as he probably would get hungry before he reached his destination. But Paquette pooh-poohed the idea, saying he could easily be there by dinner time. So off he started on his long tramp through the pathless forest, full of confidence, and never dreaming of losing his way, or deviating in the least from the straight course. Mile after mile was covered and hour after hour passed away, until both stomach and legs began to send up vigorous protests, and admonished Paquette that he was a mighty long time in getting to that shanty. However, putting on additional steam, he pressed on more vigorously than ever, and, sure enough, about the middle of the afternoon, when he was almost fagged out, and ravenous with hunger, he saw before him the welcome sight of the shanty. Hurrying up, he flung open the low door, and who should confront him as he entered but the very cook who had given him the sage advice in the morning.

"How in thunder did you get here?" said the astonished Paquette to the cook. "What the blazes brought you home so soon?" replied the still more astonished cook to Paquette. It took the latter some time to understand the matter, and to realize that, instead of travelling in what he confidently thought was a direct course to the place he intended to go, he had actually taken such a round-about, circuitous route as to arrive at the very spot he had left in the morning.

I can fully vouch for the truth of this story, and its improbability will be greatly lessened when we remember that these lumbering shanties and their surroundings are all very much alike in appearance, and that Paquette arrived at his from a direction and through an immediate location in which he had not been working, and consequently it appeared strange to him when he came back to it again.

Pete's advice is the best, in truth the only one, I know of: when you find yourself in any perplexity or bewilderment as to your whereabouts in the woods keep your head cool, sit down on the nearest log, smoke your pipe, and don't stir until you have a fixed idea in your mind as to where you are and the course you ought to take. In nine cases out of ten, the natural instinct within you, in some mysterious unaccountable manner, will bring you in safety, and sometimes most speedily, out of your dilemma.

CHAPTER XXI.

Among the Wolves.

I RECOLLECT many years ago how the very name wolf used to strike terror into my boyish heart. In fact, my earliest reminiscences of our backwoods are associated with terrible wolf stories.

In those days, and even with many people to this day, the animal is invested with a fierce, ravenous blood-thirsty character. He is the destroying demon of the wild woods. The Ishmael of the forest, neither giving nor receiving quarter from any hand. I do not believe that there is a single particle of pity, sympathy, or respect in any human breast, or for that matter in any other breast, for the wolf. And not only so but with those who are familiar with the backwoods, and know the nature and habits of the animal, is there any fear, or dread of him. He is despised as much as he is hated. The old stories of early backwoods life, and which some people are still fond of retailing if they find a credulous awesome hearer, concerning the ferocity and boldness of the wolf in pursuing and attacking his prey, whether man or beast, are now generally regarded as mythical in the extreme, and with no real foundation in fact or truth.

I am sorry if I have to disabuse the mind of my reader of any preconceived ideas he may have of the more darkly romantic character of this animal—there is nothing of the hero about him in the terrible, bloody, horror-loving sense.

This is a veracious and not a fanciful history, and I am determined to speak nothing but the plain, simple, unvarnished truth about his wolfship.

In my opinion, he is nothing but a mean, sneaking, cowardly, yelping braggart, with no more courage than an average cur of the lowest degree. He will make as much noise about you, at a safe distance, as if he were devouring forty children, and at the same time has no more pluck in him than a rabbit. In corroboration of this I would ask you—I mean you, personally, reader—if you have ever known, or heard from indisputable authority—I am speaking of course of these backwoods—of a single person, man, woman or child, who has been killed, or even torn by a wolf? I have not. In all my acquaintance with shantymen and backwoodsmen, embracing many hundreds of men most experienced and knowing in these matters, I have never met with a single case, or even heard of one, in which wolves, singly or in numbers, have attacked and injured a human being.

If all the fearful stories we have heard, about wolves and their doings, were boiled down, we question if you could distil a single drop of human blood out of the whole process. If, then, you expect to be entertained in this chapter with some hair-raising, blood-chilling stories of wolfy horrors, you will be disappointed.

My personal experience of wolves is limited to a very small area. I may say at once that I have only seen two wolves in the woods. Once when crossing a lake on the ice I met a fellow, trotting leisurely along, to whom I said "good morning" with a ball from my Ballard; whether I hit him or not I cannot say, but, at all events, it sent him to the right-about at double quick time, and he said "good-bye" to me with a prolonged howl that has rang in my ears ever since.

The other occasion upon which I had the honor of meeting with Master Lupus, was in the middle of the night, when I was camping on Middle Branch Lake. I was awakened out of sleep by the whining of my dog, a small spaniel, and a rustling and tearing among the leaves and underbrush near the camp.

Seizing my double-barrelled fowling-piece I peered cautiously out of the tent door in the direction of the noise. In the reflection of the glimmering fire, in front of the tent, I saw distinctly the lurid glare of two fiery eye-balls, not ten yards distant in the scraggy undergrowth. I knew at once it must be the wolf whose howling had kept me awake in the earlier part of the night. "I'll put you out of that, anyway," I said to myself, letting blaze at the same time both barrels straight between the shining balls of fire. The howl that followed was most satisfactory, and was repeated at intervals with devilish and excruciating emphasis, as he plunged into the deep recesses of the forest. "I haven't killed you," I said to myself, for the gun was only charged with small shot, "but at all events I have cured you of coming prowling round my tent in the middle of the night."

So much for the seeing of the brutes, but as for hearing them I have had enough of that to serve me for a life-time. The reason that you so seldom see a wolf in the woods is that, the moment he sees or hears you, he will skulk down behind a log, or into any handy covert, and remain perfectly motionless and still, until your back is turned and he thinks you are leaving him, and then he will quickly make himself heard.

The racket, and howling and snarling the wolves make in the woods, is simply terrific. If you were to judge only by it, when you hear it on every side, you would not give a penny whistle for the chance of your life. You fancy that ten thousand devils are holding high carnival in the lofty-columned halls, and under the leafy arches of the forest. It sounds as if all Pandemonium were let loose and rioting about you. I can easily understand how the blood-and-thunder stories which used to chill and curdle my young blood, and which are still greedily listened to by horror-loving ears, have their origin and plausibility. But it is all noise and nothing more—a fiendish jargon of roar and rubbish which out-clamors the tumult and hubbub of a mob of angry Chinamen or of infuriated negroes. There is not an ounce of valor in the whole mad chorus, which wakens up the echoes and makes the forest ring again, in the eerie hours of midnight.

And, yet, as you lie in your tent at night, or before the open camp fire, it is a gruesome thing to hear the wolves howling about you. At first you hear in the far distance a single distinct yelp. After a little, from another quarter, a loud prolonged howl will come suddenly echoing to your ears through the deep silence of the night, and again, and again, and again the cry will be taken up from every direction. The first is the night-call, summoning the wolves from their lairs to a rendevous from which to start on their midnight prowl and revel, and the others are the responses given in compliance with the summons. And now the noise becomes loud and furious, and as it approaches nearer and nearer you could fancy the whole forest to be alive and swarming with them, though in reality there may not be more than ten or a dozen. This is the moment when the timorous hearted and inexperienced camper will feel a strange chilly sensation about the top of his head, as if a cold air were blowing through the roots of his hair, and a queer sinking kind of collapse inside his pericardium, which causes him instinctively to examine his firearms, and heap great quantities of wood on the fire. But he soon finds that his alarm is groundless. The wolves, through some freak or other, suddenly scamper off in another direction, and their infernal din gradually lessens and dies out far away in the distance. With a sigh of relief, and thanking his stars that he is rid of them for the night, he turns in again and wraps himself up in the warm blankets.

But he is wofully deluded.

Just as he is **cosily** dropping off into sweet slumber, he hears in the far-off depths of the forest a low deep murmur. It gradually becomes louder and louder, and more distinct, until it swells unmistakably into the loud, discordant, unearthly clangor of **the** wolves. There is no doubt of it, the mad troop of howling fiends are coming direct to him again, and surely this time they will be upon him. But, like a crazy whirlwind, the pack will sweep past him, or turn off **to** the right or left, and again he will be left in peace.

The wolves seem to have **a kind of** method in their mad ranging through **the forest.** They go **in a** kind of circle or in some prescribed **course in their** nightly wanderings, and in this way pass a given point several times during the night. I have no objections to their passing as often as they please, **and** as close as they please to the camp, if they **would** only hold their tongues. But this incessantly recurring clamor completely knocks on the head all possibility of sleep.

The only thing that will bring them in close proximity to the camp, **and** keep them there too, snarling and howling all night, is the smell of any newly **killed deer that** you may have hanging near you.

The venison is quite safe, if it is hanging within the radius of the fire, or for that matter, if it is hanging anywhere, as the wolves never touch it then, or if there is any sign of human handling about it—and also if your dogs are tied near it, as they will instantly give the alarm if they approach too close.

The wolves always keep at a respectful distance from the fire, and if you don't mind their ceaseless snarling, and howls of impotent fury, you may sleep alongside of it in perfect comfort and safety.

The deer is the favorite prey of the wolf, and his ravages on this comparatively defenceless animal are frightful, particularly in the winter season, as he can travel more quickly through the snow, than the deer; and, besides, the water, in which the deer always takes refuge and through which the wolf will not so readily swim, is then frozen over and covered with snow.

In the pursuit of the deer the wolf shows great hunting tact and ability. The pack when they come upon a fresh track will spread themselves out in a line on each side of it, and on a given signal will start in pursuit—if the deer would only continue his course in a straight direction ahead, he would soon distance his howling pursuers; but this he seldom does, but bounding here and there he soon gets surrounded and is dragged down.

I have often wondered why we never find the bodies of deer who have died a natural death, as of old age or disease, or from any ordinary cause, apart from being slain. I believe the main reason of it is this: The wolves, in their cowardly way, will find out the old, weak, or sickly ones of a herd, and make them their prey to the exclusion of the others, and of course there will not be much left of the remains by the time they are done with them.

Sometimes the wolves themselves are despoiled of their prey, after they have run it down and are just beginning a jolly old feast. I have known hunters who have watched a pack of wolves chasing a deer, and so timed and intercepted them that they came up just when the deer had been pulled down, and boldly attacking the wolves, have actually snatched the carcase out of their very teeth. The fury of the brutes when thus baulked is utterly indescribable, but they are sure enough to keep their own miserable carcasses at a safe distance.

The best story of this kind I ever heard was about my old and faithful friend, Adam C.

Adam was about one of the best specimens of backwoods humanity you could meet with in a year's journey. He has lived, and hunted, and worked all his life in the woods. All his experiences and interests have been bound up and centered amid the varied and adventurous scenes of forest and river life; and a more genial, kindly heart never beat in a human breast.

One night, late in the Fall, Adam was on his way through the woods to his shanty. He was quite unarmed and alone, except a large dog that followed at his heels. Suddenly the howling of wolves broke on his ear, some distance ahead of him, and apparently of a large pack. The dog crouched to his side, and, in great terror, whined piteously. Adam, however, was not to be deterred from his course by all the wolves in the Ottawa Valley. Taking out his knife he cut a stout iron-wood cudgel, about four four feet long and two inches thick. Armed with this weapon, which, indeed, in his powerful hands, was about as formidable a one as could be conceived, he boldly advanced in the direction of the wolves, whose snarling and yelping increased in fierceness and loudness every step that he took. He had not gone far when he came upon the body of a small deer newly killed, and still bleeding, lying on the path. By the noise the wolves were making, he knew that they could not be more than thirty yards to the right hand of the spot where he was standing.

As he told me himself, such **a** racket and snapping **of teeth,** and wolf-cursing and swearing, he never heard in his life.

He guessed at once what **was in** the wind. The wolves had killed another deer at that spot, and were tearing at and fighting over it, before they came to the other one lying before him.

Most men would have been too glad to get out of such company as quickly and easily as possible. **But not so our** bold Adam. **The** deer before him **was** young, **fat** and tender, and **that deer he was bound to have. So,** hoisting it unto **his** stalwart shoulders, **he** started off on the **full** run for the shanty, from which he was still more than a mile distant. He had not gone more than half the distance, when he heard the whole infuriated pack, full **pell mell,** howling and yelling after him. Nothing daunted, **however, he** grasped his burden with a firmer hold, **and putting on** more steam, tore ahead at an **increased speed. Now** it was **that** his great staying power, and wonderful agility and strength of frame, stood him **in** good stead. The pace was something tremendous, and, when we think of it, had certainly its comical **side** in **it** ; in fact, it was a

Robbing the Wolves of their Prey.

kind of serio-comic affair altogether. It was carrying the war into Africa with a vengeance. Without doubt, it was as provoking a piece of daring impudence, on the part of **Adam**, as the wolves had ever experienced in the course of their lives. Evidently they thought so, as, with renewed clamor and increased speed, they redoubled their exertions, **when they** caught sight of the flying hunter and their bleeding **prey**.

And thus the race continued until **the** welcome **lights** of the shanty gleamed ahead, **but, at the same time, the wolves were just at** his heels, and another **bound** would bring them upon him. Adam felt that if he meant to secure his plunder he must make a *grand coup de main*. Suddenly **dropping his** burden, **with a yell and** whoop that was heard over the loudest din of his pursuers, he charged **back** upon them, and with his mighty stick dealt terrible blows right and left among them. The effect was astounding. **The** wolves, seized with a sudden panic at this extraordinary demonstration of their supposed helpless and beaten victim, with a howl **of baffled** rage, fled precipitately in every direction. Adam, taking advantage of **this** diversion, again shouldered the **deer** and bounded onwards towards the lights.

But the wolves, at the **sight of** their retreating

enemy, true to their cowardly instinct, quickly rallied, and within a few rods of the shanty again overtook him. Adam knew that it was impossible to repeat his sortie, as even his mighty reservoir of wind was about exhausted. So, dropping the deer, he bounded into the shanty and quickly rousing the men from their cards and pipes, they all sallied out with lights and axes. Charging the pack, they again harried them of their prey, and brought it in triumph to the shanty; and the wolves, with howls of baffled fury, scampered off in a panic into the depths of the forest.

I could recount dozens of stories, and true stories, too, as I can abundantly vouch for, of persons who have been followed, and chased for life as they thought, yes and treed too for hours, by these ravenous, prowling scavengers of the woods. And yet this is no evidence whatever of pluck and courage on the part of the animals, but only of ignorance and timorousness in the parties themselves. If they had not run away, the wolves would not have run after them. In fact it is characteristic of any cowardly, bullying nature, whether beast or man, to chase a flying object, and the faster the flight the more valiant the pursuit. It is just another phase of one of the meanest outcomes of human baseness, "strike him: he has no friends." All the mean yelping curs of humanity will join in the hue and cry after a running man, if only "stop thief" is shouted at him.

There is one undoubted proof of the absolutely dastard nature of the wolf, which I will give, which is almost unique in the characterization of wild animals. We have seen that even the deer, when fairly at bay, will die game, and sell his life dearly. But with the wolf it is very different. It is a well-known fact that when he is cornered up, he will skulk and whine most piteously, and allow himself to be cut and shot, and beaten to death, without a protesting snarl, or even a defiant shewing of his teeth. He dies as he has lived, an abject coward.

One short story more, and I am done with this too lengthy dissertation upon the nature and doings of the wolf.

One winter, towards evening, a shantyman was tramping through the bush carrying a load of pork on his back; suddenly the loud howling of a pack of wolves broke on his ear, and, coming nearer and louder every minute, told him that they must be in full chase after him.

Not far ahead, he knew there was an old deserted

shanty, and to it he directed his flight, as fast as his legs could carry him. He calculated his distance and saved his pork just in time. As he dashed into the shanty the wolves were just at his heels. His castle of refuge was thoroughly dismantled, nothing remained but the walls, and some of the roof beams. He saw at once that his only chance of safety was in mounting one of these beams, which was no sooner conceived of than acted upon. He had barely secured himself in a safe position, when the whole howling pack burst into the shanty. There were fourteen of them in all, and a perfect bedlam of mad wolves they were, snarling and snapping and leaping beneath him. From his vantage ground however, he could afford to laugh at them. But after a little it occurred to him that he might have something better than a laugh at their expense. He might not only turn turk upon them, but also make a pile of money out of the transaction. During the whole affair he had kept firm hold both of his load of pork, and his heavy keen-edged axe, the shantyman's inseparable companion. So lying at his full length on the beam he leaned down, and with a powerful swing of his axe by its long handle he brained the wolf that was just beneath him. This operation he repeated every opportunity he got, until finally, by occasionally shifting his position, and throwing down enticing slices of pork, he succeeded in killing the whole fourteen. At that time there was a bounty of five dollars on every wolf's head, so that the little job netted him the handsome sum of **seventy dollars.**

I give you this story, reader, just as it was told to me. Whether you believe it or not I cannot say. For my part—*I don't.*

CHAPTER XXII.

"*A Pretty Tall Snake Story.*"

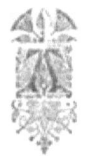HISTORY or narrative—call it what you please—such as this, would be altogether incomplete unless I said something about snakes. Snakes constitute a very important element in the economy of backwoods and river life. For many years, in common with most people, I entertained a great dread and horror of the reptiles; but that I had a good, reasonable cause for this, apart from the ordinary vulgar, superstitious repugnance to them which seems to be engrained in some people's minds, I think the following incident will abundantly show :

One bright summer morning, after an early breakfast, I, along with two young girls about my own age— we could not have been more than ten at the time—went off to gather raspberries. Our destination was an old deserted clearing full of large stones, dead logs, and thickly overgrown with raspberry bushes. It was well-known as a favorite locality for snakes, especially the common green one, which is so abundant in our back country. All this I knew right well from former acquaintance, though never so closely and unpleasantly as I was now about to experience.

While we were in the thick of our business, chatting and laughing gayly, as only children can do, especially when engaged in this pleasantest of all occupations, I suddenly felt a long, cold, clammy body creeping up the calf of my leg, and before I I could say Jack Robinson, quickly run up and round my body under my shirt. I knew at once that it was a snake. Oh, the horror of that moment! My blood and whole body seemed at once to be turned into ice. I stood transfixed to the spot. If I had been turned into a pillar of salt, like Lot's wife, I could not have been more rigidly immovable. I had read somewhere that when you are in close proximity to a snake, the best thing you can do is to do nothing, not to stir limb or muscle, but keep absolutely still. I remember well how the remembrance of this caution flashed upon my terrified consciousness, and, after one agonizing scream to my companions, I became as fixed and quiet as the rocks around me. The girls, startled by my scream, rushed towards me, and at once saw by my ghastly countenance and general appearance that there was something terribly wrong, and when I faintly whispered "snake up my leg," then the hubbub commenced in right earnest. Woman-like, they screamed and danced about me in most frantic style, and kicked up an awful flare generally. Their uproar quickly reached the ears of a man who was mowing hay in a field near by, and, with his great scythe in his hand, he was speedily on the spot.

Dan was a man who worked a great deal about the manse, and at the best of times had not the clearest intellect in the world. In his imbecile way he was very fond of me, and would run and fetch for me like a dog. What few wits he had completely left him when he understood the peril I was in. With terrible oaths and imprecations to the saints, for he was a devout Catholic, he demanded to know where the snake was. Then, joining the girls in their mad dance round me, and flourishing his immense scythe in most dangerous proximity to my body, he swore and howled alternately.

All this time the snake was having a pleasant ramble all over my body. He would run up my back between the shoulder blades until stopped by the collar band; then he would come in under my arms and dart down my sides. And every now and then he would stop and nibble at my skin; I could feel most feelingly his sharp fangs trying the cuticle, and I would say to myself: "Now I'm done for, he's going to sting me." At last I made a desperate resolve, do or die it was: just as he was crossing my chest for the twentieth time, I made a frantic clutch at his head and neck. I could feel the bones crunch in my grasp. "Now I have got him," I said, "let us go home." With my hand firmly clutching jacket, shirt, and snake, we started for the child's ever sought refuge, home and mother. A more grotesquely mournful procession never entered that village. I led the van with clenched hand in my bosom, the girls followed behind, screaming louder and louder as we neared the house, and Dan brought up the rear, making every now and then tremendous sweeps at some imaginary foe with his awful weapon.

When we arrived at the manse the family were all engaged at morning prayers, but the uproar soon brought them from their knees to the kitchen, where we had entered. And then the hub-bub commenced again. My father seized the poker, my mother got the big carving knife, and one of my sisters lifted a pot of boiling water,—what she meant to do with it neither she nor I know to this day. But finally a pair of large scissors were brought into use, and cutting through **jacket and shirt in a** large circle round my hand **the** whole piece, snake and all, was cut out, and thrown by me on the **floor**. And what **do you think after** all, reader, it turned out to be? Nothing more nor less than a small field mouse, with a long clammy tail, its body crushed into jelly in my grasp.

But, however ludicrous it may sound now, it was no joke **at the time I can tell you**; and if you ever want **to** enjoy the sensation of a snake round your **body**, just induce a field-mouse with a long moist **tail to** run **up your leg**; and I'll warrant that the sensation will tingle in your memory for many a year afterwards.

This, then, was the reason, **as** I intimated, that for many years, in fact until very lately, I felt an awful **abhorrence and** dread of **snakes**. It left such an effect on my mind that I couldn't even think of **them** without a shudder. But further experience **and** acquaintance with their disposition and habits have cured me of these feelings. As far as mere fear is concerned, I regard the whole snake family generally, I mean of course of this country, with no more antipathy than I do a caterpillar, or any other **of** the *reptilia* species.

I think it is a great pity and evil that so many

people are afflicted with such a nervous dread and abhorrence of these comparatively harmless creatures. It detracts greatly from their enjoyment of outdoor and country recreations, and, especially with women—whose hereditary dread of them has been handed down from the beginning—debars them from many of those exercises which are as invaluable for health as they are delightful in themselves.

But this is not the "tall story" that I refer to in the heading of this chapter. It is one of a much more realistic nature, though it also has its comic side, and, perhaps, is as much illustrative of certain phases of human, as of snake, nature.

The hero of this story was a young man about nineteen, who was the sole support of his family, consisting of his mother and sister and a young woman about his own age, who was a distant relation. With the latter, Jack, our hero's name, was desperately in love, and, as the sequel will shew, she warmly reciprocated the feeling; yet each was ignorant of the other's feeling on the matter, and, as the novelists tell us, in these straits, they consequently fought shy of each other, until, finally, as we shall see, the matter was most satisfactorily adjusted by the unsentimental and unromantic intervention of a black snake.

One very hot day Jack took his scythe and went off to cut wild hay in a beaver meadow, some distance from the house. These meadows are generally very retired and lonely places, and it is quite customary, when men are engaged in heavy work in them, to divest themselves of all their heavy garments, especially when the weather is uncomfortably hot,—the fact is that they often work on such occasions with nothing on but their shirt and coarse straw hat. This is the naked truth, as I can vouch for from personal observation. Now Jack, after working for a while, thought he might as well adopt this light and breezy costume, and no sooner was it thought of than, without hesitation, it was acted upon.

As he was mowing lustily away, and thinking, no doubt, about his sweetheart, and how he could propitiate her obdurate heart, he happened to tread upon a large black snake, an animal which is frequently found in the damp swampy meadows. True to its nature the snake instantly sprung, and attempted to strike its fangs into Jack's body, but missing that part which was most conspicuous, and naturally presented to him, he buried and clinched his teeth tight together in the loose flowing folds of his shirt tails, and in such a decided manner as to make it impossible for him to open his mouth, and free himself. Jack when he felt the cold clammy body strike against his legs gave one horror-stricken look backwards, and then, with a yell that made the surrounding woods echo again, he dropped his scythe, and bounded frantically from the spot, in the hope of dropping off his horrible appendage. But it was all in vain. Round and round the meadow he flew, in ever-increasing terror and speed, his shirt tail with the snake firmly locked to it by its jaws at a right angle with his back. I have often wondered whether he or the snake were the more confounded and terrified. It was certainly the most extraordinary snake drama that was ever acted on the grassy floor of that meadow. Finally Jack, in desperation, made a sudden turn, and started in a bee-line for home. As he neared the house his womankind, startled by his fearful cries of "help help, snake, snake," rushed to the door. Poor Jack was in a terrible fix, hatless, breeksless, with shirt and snake streaming behind, he didn't dare to stop. The moment he slackened his pace the hideous clammy reminder behind spurred him into fresh frantic leaps. So, bounding past the door where the horror-stricken women stood, he turned the corner, and flew round and round the house, the whole household following, with wild screams of terror and helplessness. Somebody says that "true love sharpens the wits," so it proved in this case. The young girl, when she saw Jack in peril, felt now more than she ever did before how truly she loved him, and throwing off all her coyness and reserve, with true womanly spirit and heroism she seized a large pair of sheep-shears, and stationing herself at the corner of the house as Jack passed her in his wild career, she suddenly and adroitly clipped off the shirt-tail, and delivered him from his enemy.

Needless to say, Jack and she immediately came to a right understanding, and were married before the year was out.

Now, you may be inclined to laugh at this story as being a little "too much," but it was told to me by an old grey-headed man who assured me, upon his veracity, that it was true. However, Mell, who was one of the knot of auditors, and who is a long-headed, caustic sort of fellow, and as hard of belief as the iron that he is always working among, seemed to be somewhat incredulous, "Wa'll I dunno," said he, "but I reckon its a pretty tall snake story, anyhow."

CHAPTER XXIII.

About Bruin.

SIR Bruin is a very different animal, indeed, from Master Lupus. He is a highly respectable and very formidable denizen of the forest. No one who is anyway acquainted with his character and habits is at all disposed to treat him with undue familiarity, nor approach at any but a respectful distance from him. I have heard of one man killing, single-handed, fourteen wolves, but I have known it require fourteen men to kill one bear, and even then the poor brute was shackled with a trap, and a four-foot chain attached to a heavy log.

You never hear a backwoodsman speak in disparaging terms of the bear. He knows better. One look at his knowing, peculiar physiognomy is sufficient to impress you with a high sense of his intellectual calibre. The breadth of his brain-pan, the steady, searching gleam of his small deep-set eye, his craggy, over-arching, devil-lurking eyebrow, the small, cocked, wide-awake ear, and the general contour of his sturdy, massive, self-satisfied head, neck, and shoulders, all indicate a high, and at the same time *sui generis*, order of intelligence. As he ambles along through the woods his you-had-better-let-me-alone, mind-your-own-business kind of air is provokingly fear-inspiring. You instinctivly say to yourself, " my fine chap, if I can't kill you outright with my first shot I'll not go near you."

His bearship once played a fine trick upon my friend C——and myself, at which we had many a hearty laugh at ourselves since.

We were hunting deer one day, late in the Fall, on Upper Trout Lake, when we came across the fresh track of a bear, apparently not more than an hour old. Without hesitation we abandoned the trail of the deer we were following, and gave chase upon that of the bear. Several inches of snow had fallen the night before, and the footprints were easily traceable in it. We followed the track for several hours over the roughest country imaginable, for the bear, when he finds himself pursued, always takes the most difficult and rugged course he can find. Many a fall and tumble, heels-over-head, we got in jumping the fallen trees and up-turned roots, and climbing up and down the steepest hills, as we pressed excitedly on on the ever-freshening trail. Suddenly it became so unmistakably fresh that we felt sure we were just upon him, and that before long we must tree him. Sure enough, at the foot of an immense cedar, the track abruptly stopped, and we simultaneously exclaimed, "we've got him at last." Carefully examining the ground on every side of the tree, we could discover no signs of the track, so up the tree he must be, hidden among the branches. With great glee we prepared ourselves for the coming fray. But after examining every nook and recess among the branches, we could discover no trace of his whereabouts. With utter bewilderment we gazed at the tree, and at one another. What could it possibly mean? Where in the name of all that was mysterious was he? Up the tree, or on the tree, or in the tree he certainly was not. Even a squirrel could not have concealed himself from our close scrutiny.

"By St. Hubert," said C—— "he has fooled us somehow."

Suddenly the same thought struck us simultaneously. "The rascal has gone back on his tracks," we exclaimed, almost in the same breath. A close inspection of the trail soon showed us that our conjecture was correct. The cunning old rogue had completely outwitted us. With a cool longheadedness, and a calculating judgment that would have done credit to the most knowing and expert backwoodsman, he had fairly doubled on his tracks, and was now doubtless laughing in his own grim fashion at our wild-goose chase after him.

About a mile back on the track we found where he had, in a close, thick spot, leaped to the side, and struck off at right angles to his former course. In the eagerness of our pursuit we had never noticed this divergence, nor yet the marks of his returning footsteps, for we never dreamed of his playing us such a scurvy trick.

As we had lost more than an hour in our blind futile chase, and it was near night, we were compelled to abandon the pursuit, and at our best speed, and with many a malediction on old Bruin's head, to make for camp, from which we were several miles distant.

The bear in many points of view exhibits some of the most extraordinary phenomena that are presented in the whole range of natural history: prominent among these is his habit of hibernation—a habit that has puzzled many a mind, and concerning which some very absurd ideas are entertained.

On the approach of cold weather the bear casts about in his mind for a suitable place in which to make his winter domicile. I have been **told** by Indians and others that **he** will often **ramble** a hundred **miles** before he selects a spot that will please him. His favorite location is in the heart of some dense thicket, in a cavernous hole formed at the base of an immense uprooted tree. This he can easily enlarge by throwing out the earth with his powerful paws, and soon make a deep, **warm**, roomy retreat, in which **he** makes a most comfortable bed **of** dry leaves **and moss.** I have often observed these dens in my wanderings through the bush, and they have such a dry, inviting, cosy aspect that you could almost wish you were **a** bear that you might ensconce yourself in one of them, and sleep **away** the long, dreary winter months, far removed from the hurly-burly, and heart-sickening wear and tear of human life.

Finally **lodged in** his den the bear remains **in** a dormant, semi-conscious state **until** spring, though occasionally **he** comes out for a day or two's ramble, if a heavy thaw and sunny warm weather takes place. What a jolly old sleep he must have during all these long months, and how precious hungry he **must be** when he emerges in the spring! **Yet,** strange to **say,** he comes out as fat, **some say** fatter, than when **he** entered. I suppose nobody has ever weighed him at the different periods so as to make a correct estimate. But one thing is sure, when he issues out in the spring he is not thin, as we would naturally expect, but very fat—in fact, in prime condition, both as to fur and flesh. The common idea that he lies sucking his paw, in order to appease the cravings of hunger, is all a myth. The truth is, as I have been told by hunters who have watched him through an opening in the snow, he lies on his belly, with his nose between his outstretched forepaws, just as you see a hound lying on a rug before the fire. And though his den will become completely covered over, perhaps several feet thick with successive layers of snow, still the heat generated by his warm breath and the closeness of the place, soon makes a small opening, through which the hot steam will come issuing forth, and often betrays the place to the wary hunter. In this case the bear becomes an easy prey in the hunter's hands, for in his sleepy condition he can offer but little resistance, and is either shot as he lies in his den, or knocked on the head with an axe as he is forced by smoke or dogs to issue lazily forth.

The bear, very shortly after his emergence from his winter-quarters, begins to lose his fat and fair appearance, and in two or three weeks presents such a thin, scraggy, scarecrow appearance that, to use the hunter's expression, "he is good for nothing but dog's meat."

During the period of hibernation the she-bear brings forth her young, two or three in number, though instances are known in which the birth did not take place until considerably later, sometimes well on into early summer.

The attachment of the she-bear to her young is proverbial, and during the period that they remain with her it is perilous in the extreme to annoy, or, in fact, go near her at all.

One of the most striking instances of this kind was told me by old Thomas F——, the pioneer backwoodsman of this country. It is more than sixty years since he carved out his home in this district, and of course he is thoroughly familiar with every phase of backwoods life. In his youth and middle age he was a man of extraordinary vigor and activity of body, and even yet his tall, muscular, bony frame can endure an amount of fatigue and toil which would outdo many a much younger man. He is the oracle of this community, and is as much respected for his single-minded, straight-forward honesty as he is liked for his genial, intelligent companionship. Many a stirring tale of hardship and adventure he related to me, of which the following is illustrative of the characteristic I refer to:

One day he was cutting wood in a swamp some distance from his home. He was quite unarmed, except his axe, and was accompanied by his little boy, a lad of about eight years of age, and his large dog. Suddenly he heard the dog barking furiously at a distance in the swamp. On going to the spot he found the animal engaged in fierce and clamorous combat with a large she-bear and her two cubs. The moment the enraged animal saw Tom she at once left both the dog and her cubs, and with open mouth and loud angry growls rushed at him. There was nothing for it but to beat a hasty retreat, which he did with all speed, carrying his child in his arms. The chase continued for nearly a mile, for the bear's progress was continually retarded by the dog, who at every opportunity fastened on to her flank, otherwise she would quickly have overtaken him, when certainly both Tom and the child would have fallen victims to her fury.

Finally, however, he was compelled to take refuge in a tree, into the lower branches of which he had just time to throw his child and mount himself when the bear reached the foot. Now it was that the dog's faithfulness and strength served him to good purpose. Every time the bear attempted to mount the tree the dog seized her by the haunches and dragged her down. Tom said that the fury of the animal when thus pulled down, and baulked of her prey, was fearful to witness. She would make a furious charge at the dog, and drive him off for a considerable distance, and then suddenly turn and bolt for the tree, with the expectation of getting up and out of reach before the dog could overtake her. But the noble animal, apparently divining her purpose, was always too quick for her, and would seize and haul her down the moment she commenced the ascent. Thus the battle continued for several hours. At times the maternal instinct in the bear would impel her to go off in the direction of her cubs, but the demon of rage and revenge would get the better of this feeling, and she would stop, and turn back, with greater fury than ever, to the assault, again to be baffled by the watchful and faithful dog. It was not till late in the afternoon—and it was early in the morning when Tom first saw the bear—that she finally retreated, and when he saw that she was fairly off through the bush, and courageously followed up with triumphant clamor by the gallant dog, with throbbing and thankful heart he descended from the tree, and proceeded in safety to his home.

CHAPTER XXIV.

More about Bruin.

THE respectable character and peculiar habits of the bear deserve another chapter at our hands.

There are few hunters who attempt to track the bear into the fastnesses of the forest, and hunt him there, single-handed. The uncertainties of overtaking or finding him so as to have a fair shot are in the first place so great, and the dangerous nature of the animal, if only wounded and not immediately disabled, so dreaded, that only the most expert and fearless hunters ever attempt it.

The common and favorite mode of hunting the bear, if hunting it can be called, is by trapping, either by the "deadfall" or the ordinary steel trap. The "deadfall" is a very simple contrivance, though it requires considerable dexterity so to locate and construct it as to make it effectual. It consists of a strong enclosure, built against a rock or broad trunk of a tree, of about three feet at the entrance and four feet high and deep. The trap proper consists of two heavy logs, one lying on the ground at the entrance, and the other rising from the end of it in a sloping direction, and upheld in this position by an ingenious contrivance of most insecure props. The bear, in order to get at the bait—a piece of pork or strong-smelling fresh fish—has to pass under this sloping log, and in so doing, and in pulling at the bait, is compelled to knock away the props and thus bring down upon him with great force the heavy loaded log, which either breaks his back or pins him tightly to the lower log, where he will be found by the hunter, either dead or helpless.

The steel trap of common use is a most ferocious looking instrument. It is of the same form and principle as the ordinary rat-trap, only immensely magnified in size and weight. When spread out on the ground it will measure eighteen inches between the jaws, and, along with the strong chain attached to it, weighs about thirty pounds. The bait is placed in a small inclosure made of branches or logs and open at one side; the trap is so placed, directly in front of the opening, that the bear must pass over it in order to get at the bait. The trap is completely covered over with leaves and light moss, and in such a natural manner that the spot where it lies with out spread jaws is not distinguishable from the surrounding surface of the ground. It is then securely fastened by a strong chain, of four to six feet in length, to a long heavy pole. The moment the bear, in trying to get at the bait, steps upon or even touches the broad pan in the centre of the trap, which holds the spring, the terrible jaws, teethed with sharp spikes an inch in length, snap together with the quickness of lightning, and pinion his leg in an inextricable embrace.

With a tremendous spring he attempts to free himself, and, if the chain had been fastened to a tree or any solid fixture, so great is his strength at such a moment that he would be almost certain to break it; but the pole at once yields and goes with him in the spring, and, with fearful growls of rage and agony, he bounds off through the bush, tearing away everything before him in his wild, furious career. But the heavy pole, catching upon the trees, roots, and other impediments, continually retards his progress, and at length wearies out even his mighty strength, until, finally, in utter prostration, he is brought to a halt. He may travel for miles, however, before he succumbs in despair, and is then found by the hunter, it may be some days afterwards, either dead, or helplessly entangled by chain and pole in some dense thicket, or am on fallen trees.

There are **some** queer stories told about Bruin in his attempts to free himself from the iron-grip of the trap. **It is said that he will** gnaw through his **leg just** above the **jaws of the trap, and leave** his paw and part of the limb in it, **and** then scamper off on the mutilated member. Whether this is true or not I will not undertake to say, as I have no indisputable evidence on the point. But one strange **trick** of his **I do know, and** will **stake my** veracity **upon** its frequent occurrence. When the bear finds **that he cannot** stake off his incumbrances he will deliberately climb a lofty tree, dragging chain and pole after him, until he comes to some suitable crotch or limb and throw himself over it headlong towards the ground, in the hope that his great weight will break either chain or pole, or **release him in some way.** Sometimes his manœuvre succeeds. The tendons and flesh of the leg will **be** torn out by the jerk, and the sudden strain laid upon them, and the bear **will fall to** the ground, stunned and agonized **by** the pain, but freed from his deadly fetters. Often, however, his weight is not sufficient to effect this purpose, and he will be found hanging in the air, with the pole firmly lodged in the crotch.

It sometimes happens that **the** hunter has so naturally and ingeniously covered over the trap and chain that he has difficulty in finding its exact locality, and unless he is exceedingly wary he is as likely as not to set his foot upon and be caught in his own trap.

There is a good story of this kind told about a German settler, named Switzer, who had squatted on a lot in these backwoods. Switzer had been greatly annoyed by the depredations of a large bear upon his scanty crops of corn and wheat, and though he had often lain in wait, and had had several shots at him, yet he had never hit him, or succeeded in scaring him from his premises. So he resolved to set a trap for Bruin; and so he did, and concealed it in such an ingenious manner that, going early one morning to look at it, he unwarily set his foot on the pan, and instantly the sharp-spiked jaws snapped together, and locked him fast by the calf of the leg in an iron embrace. All his efforts to release himself were utterly unavailing, for with one leg in the trap it is impossible for a man to press down the springs on both sides of the jaws, and the pole to which he had fastened the ring of the chain with nails and wedges was too heavy to drag after him on one leg. So there he was, as securely caught in his own trap as any bear possibly could be. The pain from the spikes buried in his calf was of course excruciating, but all he could do was to while away the weary hours with howls of agony and cries for assistance. In this terrible fix who should make an appearance upon the scene but the bear himself. Slowly advancing to within a few feet of the spot, he deliberately raised himself on his hind-quarters, and with his mighty forearms folded on his shaggy breast calmly surveyed the terrified prisoner. No doubt he at once took in the whole situation, and with grim satisfaction must have enjoyed it hugely. Never was a hapless mortal placed in a purgatory of greater torment than was poor Switzer. Thus, nearly the whole day passed. Every now and then the bear, with a sardonic grunt of delight, would plunge off into the woods, no doubt for provender, but would soon return and resume his squatting, watchful position, till towards evening, when he left him for good to seek his nightly lair.

In the meantime, Switzer's wife, alarmed at his protracted absence, set out in search of him, and striking his trail soon came within hearing of his frantic howls and yells. But Switzer's trials were not yet over. When his wife reached the spot, she seemed to survey the scene with as much satisfaction as her predecessor, the bear. Her husband was a man who, upon occasion, was very much given to liquor, and when in his cups was the plague and terror of her life, and now she saw that her opportunity was come. Instead of complying with Switzer's entreaties and cries for release, which had redoubled when his wife made her appearance, she calmly informed him that she would not stir one finger for his deliverance until he solemnly promised, and swore on oath before Heaven, that he would not taste spirituous liquors of any kind for the next five years. With many a grimace and protest of unwillingness, Switzer was compelled to obey and solemnly promise, and take the required oath. Whether he kept it or not I can't say, but the facts of the case, as I have told them, I can vouch for with all earnestness.

I have already spoken of the wonderful attachment which the she-bear has for her young,—an incident illustrating this, and, at the same time, the well-known sagacity of the animal, occurred while I was in this country, and was related to me by an eye-witness. A bear with three cubs was discovered by some axemen in the woods, and, taking flight, was hotly pursued by them. She could soon have outdistanced them, had it not been for the cubs, who were of too tender an age to run with any speed; but the motherly instinct within her would not allow the bear to desert her offspring; so every time a cub would become wearied and lag in the flight she would thrust her nose under the little fellow and give him a tremendous heave ahead of her, and then follow up with redoubled speed. This she kept up continuously with the three, one after another, and thus contrived to keep herself and them at a safe distance from her pursuers. "It was astonishing," my informant told me, "how quickly the little fellows understood the stratagem of the old dame, and if one happened to fall out of the line of flight would immediately place himself in the right position for another toss." I was delighted beyond measure to be told, as I am sure you are too, reader, that the brave, loving old mother succeeded in saving herself and her cubs, in spite of the utmost exertions of her pursuers.

I have been told, and I have no reason to doubt the truth of the statement, that when a bear is badly wounded, and seeks for safety in flight, that he will, after running swiftly for a time, deliberately stop and endeavor to staunch the bleeding of the wound by leaves and damp moss.

If, reader, you ever find yourself in close quarters with a bear, and have no gun or revolver with you, pick up the first stone or stick that is handy, and strike him a blow with all your might fair on the snout, and ten to one you will rout and vanquish him. A good story in proof of this was told me by the head clerk of my friend C——'s concern. He was once furiously charged by a bear, and so suddenly that he had no time to pick up stone or stick. Remembering this sensitive spot of the animal's body, he made a quick counter-charge, and planted such a lusty kick with his heavy top-boot in his nose and mouth that he knocked in all his front teeth, and so appalled the brute that, with a howl of agony, he instantly changed his furious charge into an ignominious and precipitate flight.

I conclude this subject of the bear by relating an incident told me by Adam C——, the hero of the wolf story. At the risk of wearying the reader, I give this incident on account of its peculiar, and, to me, utterly inexplicable, exhibition of some feelings and traits of bear nature and habits which I believe have never yet been recorded and explained. One evening Adam was travelling through the bush, when, from a small eminence on which he stood, he saw, about eighty yards before him, a large bear, busily engaged in pawing among the dead leaves for nuts. He fired at the animal, and apparently severely wounded him, for he immediately fell, and, rolling over, growled in convulsive agony. Without stirring from his position, he proceeded—as every experienced hunter does—to reload his gun. While thus engaged he saw, to his no small alarm, no less than five bears plunging, one after another, out of the bush, and joining their wounded brother. The furious uproar and clamor that at once ensued was perfectly appalling, and quickly decided Adam to take to his heels as fast as he could, and he was so terrified that he never halted in his flight until he arrived at the shanty. The next morning, accompanied by several of his men, well armed with guns and axes, he proceeded to the spot. And such a scene of wild havoc and furious rage he never witnessed. The ground was dug into and turned up as if it had been roughly ploughed; immense stones had been torn out, and the bark and wood of the surrounding trees was hanging in shreds from the trunks. No trace of the bear he had shot could be seen until, on further examination, they found the trail where the bears had gone off in a body, and, strange to say, had dragged with them the dead or disabled body of their companion. They could distinguish this from the blood on the ground, and the hairs which had been rubbed off on the logs and roots over which they had to cross. They continued the pursuit for several hours, when want of time compelled them to abandon it. I leave this singular incident to the understanding and explaining of those who are wiser and better posted in bear nature and habits than I am. And so, farewell to Sir Bruin and his eccentricities!

Recreation.

CHAPTER XXV.

The Breaking-up of the Ice.

THE breaking up of the ice, which is always accounted the true advent of Spring, is an event long looked for and eagerly desired by the shantymen.

For two or three weeks preceding it there is a breathing-time of comparative idleness to the men. The heavy work of the woods is finished. The cutting, sawing and hauling are all over for another season. The square timber and sawlogs are lying many tiers deep on the ice, or piled up on the bank, waiting for the rising water and bursting of the ice to be swept down the river.

It is an anxious time for the foremen and manager; for upon a favorable and early start, with a good "pitch of water," may depend the whole success of the " drive." If the ice "hangs on" too long the water may fall—in fact, it is falling every day after a certain pitch—and unless it is taken at a good flow the timber will get " stuck," or, if not, will involve greatly increased labor and expense in driving the small streams and rivers before it is fairly launched on the broad, deep bosoms of the Ottawa and St. Lawrence. When once afloat in these majestic rivers it is safe, and then, hurrah for Quebec! with all available speed of wind and steam, for the sooner to market the less expense of food and wages, and the better chance of speedy and high "prices."

During this season of enforced inactivity the foremen are often at their wits' end what to do with the men. With their characteristic energy and push they hate to see them loafing and smoking round the shanty. Provisions are vanishing at inverse progression to the work done, and high wages are all the time running on. Of course those who were engaged only for the winter have been paid off and have gone to their homes and farms, but the men who were hired "for Quebec," and the new hands engaged for the "drive" are all on the spot, lying on their oars, waiting for the breaking up of the ice.

This is the time for the "green hands" to exercise themselves on the loose timber and logs. The boys who have never been down the river before go into training now for the slippery, hazardous work ahead of them. With pikepole and handspike, they go leaping from log to log, and many a dip over the head they get in the ice-cold water.

I was immensely amused one morning in watching the *manœuvres* of a droll character called Ferdinand. Ferd was a short, fat, jocund, good-natured Frenchman. I always thought he was a German, till informed otherwise. I believe in truth, however, he must have got mixed up somehow in the Franco-German war, for, though undoubtedly French, he had all the characteristics and appearance of a full-blooded Teuton. He was about as good-humored a soul as I ever met with. It was as natural for him to laugh as for water to ripple in the breeze; in fact, his face was a perpetual grin, an everlasting wrinkle of jollity. You couldn't look at the man without feeling happy. His presence was a contagion of merriment which completely annihilated all thoughts of the tomb—Death's head and he were sworn enemies.

Ferd, who had never been on loose timber before, thought he would try his feet on it this morning along with the other boys. In his easy-going way, he hopped about from stick to stick, apparently in great conceit with himself, and no doubt thinking it no great matter after all "to go on timber." Now a stick of square timber or a sawlog floating loose in the water is the most deceitful institution under the sun, and, though you may fancy yourself for a little to be quite secure, still, if it gives the slightest "cant," or roll to the side, you feel at once you are in a most precarious position, and unless you are up to the thing, ten to one you are certain to go over. So it turned out with honest Ferd—he finally landed on a log, which, true to sawlog nature, began to revolve rapidly in the water. Ferd evidently thought he had got on the wrong log, for he at once displayed marked signals of distress, and, not knowing that, in order to preserve his balance, he must keep pace with his feet with the revolutions of the log, he was plunged head-foremost into the icy water, and nothing was to be seen of him but the soles of his boots wabbling above the surface. As he emerged and scrambled up like a broken-winged duck on to a firm stick, his loud spluttering, "wah, wah, hoo, hoo," could be plainly heard above the wild cheers of merriment and derision with which he was greeted by his companions.

"Dat was a fine christening for your work, Joe," the foreman consolingly shouted to him, when he had regained his balance. Ferd tried to keep up a good face, but it was no use; his habitual good-humor had received a decided quencher, and with a grin on his countenance, about as merry as that of a skull, he bolted for the shanty as fast as his wet clothes and short legs would allow him.

During this season of inaction it is certainly more amusing than instructive to listen to the wise men of the backwoods, as they discourse sagely on the signs of the coming spring. Each one has some infallible sign in which he places implicit confidence; and this he will enunciate with a gravity and assurance that lends a kind of preternatural sapience to his prognostications. They out-vennor Vennor, in the minuteness and particularity of their weather wisdom. I have listened to more rank nonsense in this connection than in any other matter to which I ever gave my attention. In our variable, uncertain and capricious climate, I often think that our best wisdom is to keep a shut mouth about the weather; at any rate to be excedingly modest and diffident in expressing our opinion, even as to the "probabilities" on the question. However, I will mention some of those signs, just as I heard them, and, reader, " thou shalt be judge."

Six weeks ago there was every appearance of a complete breaking up of the winter. A heavy thaw was succeeded by warm rains and a bright, hot sun. The snow all disappeared—the ice became rotten, and the frost was all out of the swamps. Humanly judging, the Spring was just upon us. Now was the time for signs. Never was there a more opportune season for the soothsayers and interpreters. Joe had seen a chipmonk playing about the shanty. "No mistake this time," said he, " I never knew this sign to fail for sure." The chipmonk burrows in the ground, and dens up during the cold winter months. Old Sarcon, whose grey hairs and experience demanded respect and attention, had heard wild geese flying North the night before; and another worthy had seen five of them beside a small pool on the ground. A ground-hog had issued forth from his winter-quarters and had been worried by a dog; crows, robins, phœbes, whippowills—birds innumerable—all sure harbingers of Spring, had been seen and heard. Sawwhets had been heard in the bush in the dead of night. This strange, weird, mysterious sound, whether of bird, or animal, or tree, or demon, no man knows, resembling somewhat the sharpening of a saw, is one of the hyper-infallibles in the sign business. And so on, and on, the same old story ran.

It was the continual topic of discourse round the camboose, and accompanied with such grave portentous nods of the head, and solemn, emphatic assever-

Tom, the Philosopher,

ations that you felt ashamed of yourself for feeling any doubt or uncertainty on the question.

But, alas, for both human and brute intelligence, and boasted understanding of the deep subject of weather, all these learned disquisitions and opinions began and ended in signs. Winter with all its rigor came back upon us just as suddenly as it had left us, and in much more severe mood. Hill and valley, forest and lake were covered with a snowy carpet nearly a foot deep. The rivers were again bound in icy fetters, and the marshes and swamps were tightly frozen up. Winter again reigned supreme, and all nature laughed aloud at the vain attempt of the wise men to solve the mysteries of her designs, and unlock the secrets of her workings.

"What do you think of all this?" I demanded of an old friend of mine, who walked about among us with the lofty air of a Field Marshal of the Old Regime, and who was familiarly designated by us, as "Tom the Philosopher." With Confucian sententiousness, he gave an answer worthy of the Master, "I believe in Spring when I see the grass growing, and the swallow flying."

Now, in all seriousness, I believe there is a great deal of nonsense written about the so-called infallible instinct of animals in interpreting the phenomena of

s

their surroundings, so as to know what kind of weather and climate are ahead of them. I think they are as often deceived in these matters as we are, that their judgments are as shortsighted and superficial, and the outcome of mere appearances and of local and temporary sensations, as those of the ordinary run of human intelligences. In other words, they are no better weather prophets than we are.

However, I have no intention of philosophizing on this or any other subject in this book, and I simply remark that, be this as it may with regard to the animals themselves, at all events, one thing is certain, *we* make egregious mistakes when we calculate as to the probabilities of the weather on the actions, movements, and supposed instinct of these animals, as is clearly shown not only in the cases I have just spoken of, but in almost every recurring season of the year. *The animals may be right absolutely,* as far as the conditions and necessities of the narrow circle in which they move and were designed for, are concerned (and what more do they require?) but *we are wrong* in our interpreting and understanding of them to suit our own purposes.

When the ice is fairly broken up, and the vast flotilla of logs and timber is actually on the move, then we have one of the most lively and interesting scenes of river life.

The vast accumulations of snow and ice which have been formed during the winter are now rapidly melting and disgorging by a thousand foaming rivulets into stream and river, and all combined are hastening to pay their annual tribute in ever-increasing volume to the great mother ocean, which embosoms the world.

The deep river beds are now not only filled to their utmost capacity, but where the ground is low-lying, in swamp or marsh, the country on both sides is completely submerged, forming what are called "lagoons" in the Southern States, and in our backwoods "drowned lands." In such conditions, the river often presents the appearance of a vast lake on which, among the black ash and willows, the timber and logs float at their "own sweet will."

The first business of the drive is to collect all these scattered timbers, and "boom" them into the main channel of the river, that is, confine them there by long half-square logs called "boom timber," fastened at the ends by "boom chains." These will sometimes line the true banks of the river for miles at a stretch and effectually prevent any waywardly inclined timber from straggling into the adjoining submerged regions.

Now the "drive" has fairly commenced, and all

is life, and stir and activity on the river. It is hard work from earliest dawn to late sunset, and cold work too, often up to the waist in the icy waters for hours at a time. But it is work that is brimful of excitement and perilous interest, and exerts such a strange fascination upon those who engage in it that, with all its perils and hardships, they are always willing to re-engage on the next recurring season.

CHAPTER XXV.

A Backwoods Schoolmaster of the Olden Time.

EVEN in the remotest sections of the backwoods the school system is very different now from what it used to be, and the teacher is a different type from that of the olden time. Of course, the system is vastly improved—over-improved, I think, in comparison with the capacity of the scholars, and the pockets of the parents.

The standard of education that is insisted upon now, both for teacher and pupil, is, I think, far too high for many of our school sections in the purely rural districts, and decidedly so for our isolated backwoods. I have no hesitation in speaking strongly on this point, for I have seen the evils of it, and they require to be seen in order to be understood in all their significance. This high standard necessarily implies high salaries, for young men and women will not pass through the lengthy and arduous studies needed for the required certificates without expecting and demanding adequate remuneration.

Consequently, in many of our poor and thinly-populated school sections, where it is absolutely impossible to pay such teachers a fair and reasonable salary, one of two things follows: either the schoolhouse is closed altogether, and the children are deprived of all educational advantages, or two sections adjoining one another unite in supporting one teacher, thus giving the children only half-time education. Of course half a loaf is better than no bread, but the evils of such a system are great and manifold, and at once understood by those who know anything about educational matters. Let me instance a case in point: In the immediate vicinity of this district, in which I have pitched my tent for several months, there are two schoolhouses, four miles apart (though I think it is nearer five), between which one teacher divides her time. She teaches in the morning at one place, then takes her dinner and walks the four miles to the other school for her afternoon's work. She stays there all night, teaches in the morning, and then walks back to the former place to teach and stay for the next twenty-four hours. I have often pitied these young ladies, and many a time I met them on their long weary walk between the two schools; in every phase of the execrable weather of our fall, winter and spring, in hail, in sleet, in rain, in snow, up and down the highest hills,—it had to be done, else complaint and reduction of pay followed ; and a great part of the time the schools are vacant, just from the absolute impossibility of getting a teacher who has come up to the required standard.

I think there ought to be a discriminating certificate of attainment for isolated and peculiarly situated school sections, and I am confirmed in this opinion by the well-known fact that a high standard of attainment does not necessarily imply a high standard of efficiency in teaching. Many of our third-class certificate teachers were most successful instructors, and greatly respected and beloved by pupils and parents. However, I have gone much further in this direction than I at all intended, and, in speaking as I have done, have not the slightest intention of throwing any reflection upon our school system generally ; for, taking it all in all, I hold that it is one of the very best, and most practically efficient, in the world.

But, as the title of this chapter intimates, I wish to speak about ye olden time teacher and their system. What a mighty change has been wrought, what a different class they are now from that of thirty, forty, or fifty years ago ! How many of my readers at the thought will conjure up old memories of strange, eccentric, oddly-fashioned, **antiquated men, who** then **filled the** chairs of learning in the rural and backwoods districts? As a class they are now absolutely extinct, but are there not some among them, reader, whose **memory you** and I will not willingly let die? **With all** their **uncouth** eccentricities, their many excellencies **will** always keep them fresh and green in our recollection. Prominent among these, as the most characteristic **type that** I ever knew or heard **of, stands out old** Robert Mason, the first school**master of the** village of Lanark, between **thirty** and **sixty years ago. He was the first to whom I went to school, and I was a mere child at the time, yet** my **remembrance of him is as** fresh **and vivid as of** yesterday.

He was sent out **by the Imperial** Government with **the** first band **of immigrants (Paisley** weavers) **who settled in this country in** 1821, and for nearly **thirty years he taught and thrashed in** the little **stone schoolhouse of the village. He was a tall,** gaunt, **rawboned, beetle-browed Scotchman, an elder in the** Kirk, **and a** true-blue **Presby**terian **of** the hardest and sternest cast. He **was a man** of grave **and** serious demeanor. He **seldom smiled, and when he** did, it **was as if under protest from his** grim and iron nature. He was, withal, an exceedingly irascible old man ; and from his long tenure of office, without hindrance or interference from anyone—for there was no board of trustees in those days, nor did any one dare to counsel or censure—he had become despotic and severe to the last degree. He was just as absolute, and upon occasions tyrannical, in his sway as any autocrat of the Middle Ages.

His system of education was of the simplest and most rudimental nature. Reading, spelling, writing and "countin'" made up the sum total of his instruction. Grammar, geography, history, composition were as tongues unknown.

I remember one peculiar theory he held with regard to teaching arithmetic to girls ; he gravely maintained that there was not the least use of their going further in "countin'" than the four simple and compound rules of addition, subtraction, multiplication and division. Their minds were not capable of rightly grasping anything beyond these, nor indeed would a further advance in this branch of learning be of any practical advantage to them in after life. Hence, when some ambitious, clever-minded girl found herself just on the threshold of simple proportion, and was longing to pass its mystic portals, she was peremptorily ordered back to simple addition and the multiplication table.

The boys however were soundly drilled (for the old man was thorough as far as he went) up to vulgar fractions, but decimals, and the square and cube roots were a *terra incognita* to the " Maister," and of course to his pupils.

As I have intimated, he was severe in his code of discipline—severe! did I say ?—that is no word for it. His castigations and punishments were simply horrible, yea fiendish. I firmly believe that the old man thought, and had as an honest, conscientious conviction in his soul, that the beginning and end of all sound and effective imparting of knowledge lay in the tips of the taws. Whatever his theory was, this was his practice anyhow, I don't believe that more terrible thrashings were ever inflicted, either in ancient or modern times, than what those unhappy youths had to undergo in that old square stone schoolhouse in the village of Lanark, at the merciless hands of old Robert Mason. His taws were the most horrible instrument of torture that could be imagined. Leather was dear in those days, and as the taws were stolen at every possible opportunity that occurred, the " Maister " found it too costly a business to go to the shoemaker every

time he required a new pair, so he would rummage
round the barnyards of the neighbors until he would
find an old horse trace which had been thrown
away, and had been drying and hardening in the sun
for months. Then his soul would be delighted, and
he would forthwith fashion it into the direst weapon
of castigation that the heart of man or demon
could devise. He would pare down one end of it so
that he could conveniently wield it with both hands,
and the other end he would slice into three or more
tails and then singe and harden them in the fire to
give them more weight and sting. With this awful
weapon, perhaps five feet in length, in his hand he
would go to work as deliberately as a man in
chopping down a tree. I have seen as many as a
dozen pupils ranged before him, each waiting in
gloomy silence his turn to undergo chastisement. If
it was in warm weather each one as he came forward
had to lay his hand down on the cold stove (which
was never removed summer or winter) and then
after a long deliberate wipe of his forehead, shaggy
eyebrows, nose, mouth and chin, with his left hand
he would bring down the taws upon the hand of the
luckless culprit with a mighty pegh ! just as you
hear a man give with every swing of the axe into
the tree before him. After each one had received

his dozen or more allotted " licks " the old man would be somewhat exhausted, but I believe it was a pleasant kind of exhaustion to him, and kept him in good humor for hours afterwards.

There were about seventy of us, of all ages, from the child at his A B C up to the stalwart man of twenty or more, packed together in that small building of twenty feet square ; but Mr. Mason was no respector of ages in the distribution of his castigating favors. The tallest and stoutest youth had to come forward and lay his hand on the stove, and take his punishment with as much meekness and submission as the smallest urchin.

However he didn't have it all his own way with these big fellows ; with a kind of sullen desperation as to consequences they would sometimes revolt, and bid defiance to the old Dominie. Suddenly turning up their coat-sleeves, and spitting on their hands, they would square up to him, and call out, " Maister, I'll fecht you." Then would ensue a scene of uproar and excitement in that school that beggars all description. The " Maister," nothing loath, for he was a very powerful man, and as good with his fists as he was with the taws, and quite assured in his mind as to the issue of the combat, would calmly except the challenge, and, rolling up his sleeves, at it the two would go in down right earnest.

There was one fellow in particular who stands out distinctly in my memory as a prominent hero in these battles. Charlie was a strong, tall, big man of over twenty, the bully not only of the school but of the village also. He was an incorrigible dunce, as dense a blockhead as ever entered a school door. He neither would nor could learn anything; consequently, there was a continual feud between him and the master, and many and fearful were the thrashings he received. Occasionally, however, his stolid spirit would assert itself, and he would defy and turn on the master with the fury of a wild boar, "Maister I'll fecht you," would come sputtering from his mouth, and then the battle would commence. This was always a grand occasion for the rest of us, and, knowing that the master's attention was fully taken up, there would come from every corner of the school our rallying cries to the combatants, "weel dune, Charlie, weel dune," "bully for you, Maister," "tak' him under the leg Charlie," etc., etc. But the issue of the combat was always the same, as it generally is in such cases of dispute between teacher and scholar, Charlie would have to succumb and go to the floor, and the master kneeling on his back, and holding him down with his left hand on the back of his neck, would call loudly for his taws; at this juncture Charlie would invariably cry out "fair play, Maister, fair play, dinna strike a man when he is doun." And this appeal to the old man's generosity and honor was always effectual. With a grim smile of sardonic triumph he would allow Charlie to get up and go to his seat, and with a long self-satisfied wipe of his grave lantern-jawed countenance he would stalk in solemn dignity to his desk, and peace and quietness would again prevail. Fancy for a moment such a scene taking place in one of our schools now!

A most characteristic incident of Charlie and the master occurred about this time, which I must record. The master had just given Charlie a tremendous beating, which he underwent with such stolid ox-like indifference that the old Dominie's ire was quite unappeased, "eh, my mon," said he, "I'll bring something the morrow that will mak' ye smart."

The next morning, before school time, Charlie happened to be in the woods near the school-house, and came across the old man tugging away with all his might at a strong maple sapling about an inch thick and six feet long.

"What are gaun to do wi' that, Maister," said Charlie.

"Eh, my mon, ye'll find that out soon enough," was the angry reply, as he tugged away more fiercely than before at the sturdy sapling.

"Aw weel, I'll gie ye a haun at it anyway," said Charlie, and so he did, and between them they soon tore it up by the roots.

The Dominie was observed several times during the day to eye Charlie very curiously, and with a kind of mystified uncertain grin on his solemn countenance, but Charlie was not called up, and for some days was allowed to get off Scot-free for his delinquencies.

There was another youth in that school, Bill M——, who was quite as incorrigible as Charlie, but he was no dunce, I can tell you. His was a case of "would not" learn, without question. Though he was only twelve, the floggings he received were something terrible; but lay on as long and as heavy as he pleased, the master could never wring a groan or a tear out of Bill.

One day, however, the master's rage passed all bounds, and in a paroxysm of fury, he seized Bill by the ear with an iron grip and dragged him to the door, and passing out he went down through the street of the village, hatless and raging, his long grey hair streaming in the wind, until he reached his father's office, and still holding Bill by the ear, he thrust him into his presence, "there," said he, "there is your neer-do-weel of a son, never let me see his face again in the Lanark schule." Bill, however, was back again next day in his seat, and things went on as if nothing unusual had occurred. The old man never kept up his resentment, but allowed it to die with his temporary passion.

Charlie has long since been laid under the sod, but Wm. M—— now occupies, and for many years has occupied, one of the highest and most lucrative positions in the Bank of Montreal, and is respected and loved by all who truly know him. His four brothers also, who for longer or shorter periods passed through the same severe school of discipline, have all become settled in life as successful and promising men. One of them, a physician in Winnipeg, has attained high eminence in his profession, and the other three, as merchants, are gradually winning their way to wealth and independence.

But of all the boys who at that time were afflicted with the visitation of the rod, perhaps Chas. M—— had to undergo the severest ordeal. Charlie's besetting sin was truant—playing; he hated the school with a perfect and undying hatred, and it was only under the direst compulsion that he ever was there at all; and I can safely **aver that** all the mental and scholastic attainments that he gained during that period were absolutely *nil*. And yet a brighter genius never attended a Canadian village school than Chas. M——, which has been abundantly shewn by his career since. His life at that time strikingly resembles the early days of Thomas Edward, the celebrated Scotch naturalist. Like him Charlie would seize every opportunity to steal away to the woods, the hills and the river side, where the terrors of school and of home would be utterly forgotten. The moment his absence was discovered, a special messenger would be dispatched to his father, and if he was not at home two stalwart youths, whose faithfulness or cowardly obsequiousness could be relied on, would be sent to hunt him up and bring him to the school, and if they were successful, then dire and woeful would be Charlie's tribulations.

Charlie's father was the village merchant, and a man of the purest, thoroughbred Lowland Scotch type. He had, in common with the dominie, an utter abhorrence of the sin of truant-playing. He regarded it as one of the most deadly of all youthful sins, and to be dealt with by the most severe and merciless application of the taws. It was quite a common thing to see him appear at the schoolhouse door, leading Charlie by the hand; and, stalking up to the desk with stern aldermanic dignity, he would say: "There, Maister, tak him, and thresh the deevil out of him."

Charlie has fought his way well in the world, since he left old Lanark. As a poet and journalist he has highly distinguished himself. "The Song of the Pines," which appears in his volume of poems, entitled "Dreamland," is, as a minor production, the finest that has appeared in the whole range of Canadian literature. But Charlie has found out that Canadian literature is neither appreciated nor remunerated by Canadians themselves. Any foreign rubbish that has the imprimatur of a name upon it is eagerly bought up and read, while their own countrymen, of many of whose works they ought to feel proud and honored in the possession, are coldly and contemptuously passed by. So Charlie, like a wise man, cast literature to the dogs, and threw himself into business, and after a twelve years' successful career in the North-west has gained wealth and independence. He purposes, however, to resume his literary efforts, and I have no doubt, now that he is independent and affluent, his works will be greatly appreciated and honored by his countrymen.

I have said that Mr. Mason was an elder in the kirk, and whatever might be his failings as a teacher— and they were those of the times as much as of the individual—in this capacity he stands forth as a shining and venerated model to the most zealous and distinguished of his successors and brethren even of the present day. His sterling, unflinching integrity, his simple-minded, pure hearted piety, his practical orthodoxy, his rigid, unbending, iron-cast character, all stamped him as a man of mark and most wholesome influence in church matters, during his day and generation.

For three or four years between the resignation of Mr. Macalister and the settlement of my father, there was a vacancy in the church. During all that time Mr. Mason summoned the people sabbath after sabbath to church, and kept up a regular service. He never presumed to enter the pulpit, nor give any of his own prelections; but from the precentor's desk, after praise and prayer, would read a sermon from some old Scotch worthy.

It was during this period that the disruption in

Scotland took place, and, as every one knows, the dark and angry winds of confusion and strife were blown across the waters to this country, and rent and troubled the church in every corner of the land. Lanark, of course, did not escape, and being vacant was looked upon as a particularly inviting field for the operations of the secessionists. So Dr. Burns, who had been going up and down through the country, inflaming all hearts, and overturning all opponents by his fiery, stormy eloquence, came, and in his imperious maner, demanded entrance into the church for the following sabbath. But he had met his match for once. "Na, na," said old Robert to him, "ye'll never pit your foot in yon pulpit while I have the key of the kirk in my pocket."

The Sabbath morning came, and there was a great stir and commotion among the people, I can tell you. The grim, brave, old elder took his stand at the church door, and on every side was a great concourse of people. When the Doctor appeared he defied him to enter, and bade him depart and trouble Israel no longer. The Doctor saw at once, of course, that there was no admission there for him except over Mason's dead body, so he betook himself to the old wooden courthouse, which stood on the hill just in the centre of the village, and thither all the multitude flocked, and with them old Robert, with no very worshipful thoughts, I fancy.

The building was packed to its utmost capacity, and surrounded on all sides by an excited throng. The Doctor, fully expectant of a grand triumph over the old elder and the kirk, had finished the preliminary services, and was proceeding with his sermon. With all the force of his fiery eloquence, and burning wrath, he was declaiming against the iniquities and corruptions of the Church of Scotland, when suddenly, old Mason, who was sitting directly in front of him, with his keen steel-grey eyes gleaming like meteors through his shaggy, over-arching brows, rose to his feet, " I canna staun that, I canna staun that!" he burst out, and with a stamp of his massive foot on the floor, which shook the building to its foundation, he strode down the aisle to the door. The terrible earnestness of the old man, his unmistakably righteous wrath, his stern, impressive, commanding demeanor, utterly disconcerted the Doctor in his impassioned flow of denunciation and abuse, and completely spoiled any effect which might have been made upon the people. And it is a historical fact that, though all the churches in the neighborhood were in a blaze, and many of them left the old kirk at the time, yet there was not the slightest defection in the church at Lanark; and though many vigorous attempts were made, both then and subsequently, yet from that time there was not the smallest foothold or encouragement for the Free Church obtained.

The brave, honest, manly, old Dominie has long since been gathered to his fathers, and his scholars are scattered far and wide over the face of the earth; but I believe that the impress of his truthful, sturdy, determined character has been imprinted upon many of them, and has in no small degree moulded them for good, and fitted them in a large measure for the stern, hard battle of life.

CHAPTER XXVI.

Jams.

READER, have you ever seen a genuine, fair and square, up-and-down, orthodox "jam"?

If you have not, then you have yet to see one of the grandest sights which our backwoods river life can afford. It is a scene that cannot be painted or described aright. It must be witnessed in order to appreciate rightly and fully its perilous excitement, its complicated movements, its hazardous handling, its sudden bursting, and the wild hurryscurry leaping and hurrahing of the men as they make their escape to the shore over the heaving, gliding, rolling timbers. It is a mimic battle between men, logs, and water, and occasionally lasts for a week at a time before human strength and skill carry the day.

Jams are of very frequent occurrence on the river, though some spots are particularly notorious for their difficulty and danger in this respect, and have repeatedly been the scenes of terrible accidents to life and limb. Consequently, when they are approached, the most experienced, skilful, and active hands are stationed to watch and guard against them. These places are commonly called "chutes," and are generally narrow, crooked, and precipitous descents of the river, forming, consequently, foaming and turbulent rapids, and frequently terminating in most dangerous eddies and whirlpools.

A short distance above the place a strong "boom" is laid across the river in order to keep back the timber, and "knowing hands" are stationed here to let it out gradually, a few sticks at a time; so that the timber may not crowd or float too thickly into the rapids. Behind this "boom" the whole "drive" is generally collected before they proceed to run the "chute," and the whole force of men is concentrated on the various points of difficulty, in order to force the timber through. In spite of all precautions however, jams, and tremendous ones too, will take, place. Some refractory stick, generally some worthless "cull," or rotten, twisted piece that is hardly worth taking to market, is the cause of the whole mischief. Just as it is in human associations, it is often the most useless, cranky member of society, who will not run smoothly, and according to book, that causes the greatest trouble and damage among his followers. So there are "cranks" among the timber which can neither take care of themselves nor yet keep out of other sticks' way. They will run broadsides, or any way but the right way, in the most ticklish part of the chute, and will be sure to stick at the very place where they ought to run the quickest. Before the man who is stationed at this spot can dislodge such a stick, for it suddenly developes a leech-like attachment to the place, others have crowded down, and, though all the available force in the immediate vicinity is summoned to bear upon it, yet a jam is formed which increases in tightness and solidity with every fresh stick from above.

The men are very loath in such circumstances to pass the alarm to the hands on the boom—perhaps nearly a mile above—not to pass through any more timber, and will tug, and pry, and heave, with every muscle and energy at the utmost strain, in order to loosen the wedged-in, tightly-packed mass. In the meantime the timber from above is "driving" rapidly down, and every stick strikes against the jam with the violence of a battering-ram, and wedges it in more tightly still. Meanwhile the rushing, boiling waters of the narrow gorge will be rapidly damming up and pressing down on the confined bound timbers with inconceivable force.

Without doubt, a jam—a veritable old-fashioned, no humbug jam—has been formed, and it will take "all hands and the cook" to loosen it.

A wild and exciting scene of bustle and activity now takes place. Every man is on the alert, and throwing his whole strength into the work. The only man who is cool and collected is the foreman, and he needs to be; if ever experienced and calculating judgment, as well as nerve and ability, is required, now is the time. As soon as he finds out the salient points of the jam, and above all the *pièce de resistance*, he attacks it with all his force and skill. With wild whoop and yell the men respond to his summons, and go at it with a will.

As you stand on the shore and watch the scene you are imbued with a strange, restless, feverish excitement. You can't remain still, you must move in unison with the men before you, and involuntarily you find yourself joining in with their wild shouts and hurrahs, as some temporary advantage is gained.

It is astonishing how the men are animated and assisted in their work by the peculiar cry of their foreman. It is like the "tally-ho" with the hounds. "Héé Yo; Héé!" it is, with a clear, ringing, musical measure which can be heard a mile away. If given

Letting off the Water.

with the right emphasis and intonation it will so concentrate the energies of the men that fifty or a hundred of them will pull and pry as one man.

But the climax of interest in this scene is when the jam is giving way and bursting; with the crash and noise of thunder it sweeps away everything before it, and in a furious, whirling, seething jumble of logs, up-rooted trees, and foaming torrent, rushes down the gorge with lightning speed. Every man has now to look out for himself, and make for the shore the best way he can. As they leap from stick to stick, in the tumbling, whirling mass, it is almost miraculous how they escape. And as they go bounding along, every man is whooping at the pitch of his voice, "There she goes, There she goes, Hoorah! Hoorah!" and, with a wild scramble and yell, they are all safely ashore, and the danger and excitement are over for this time.

Some of the most narrow escapes from mutilation and drowning are of everyday occurrence during the driving season. One of the most remarkable of these that I ever heard of was one in which Duncan the manager, was the principal participant.

He was driving a raft of timber on the Mississippi, when a formidable jam occurred a short distance above the bridge, at Innisville. This is a very dangerous place, and **was** rendered particularly **so** that year by the unusually **swollen** state of the river, consequent upon the bursting of one of Gilmour's dams at the foot of Crutch lake. The main portion **of the** jammed timber had been **all** safely got off, and down the stream, **but** the "tail" still remained firmly lodged in the very centre of the rapids, and in the most dangerous **place.** Duncan saw that **two men** were all that were required to take it off, **and** looked about for some **one to select for** his companion. He must have **a man upon** whom he could thoroughly rely in every respect, as the undertaking **was of the most** difficult and dangerous character. **One man was anxious to** go with him, but, though competent in **every respect,** Duncan, **at a** glance, saw that he had been "swiping" too freely.

In those days liquor was most plentifully used **on** the drive. Whenever they came to those places involving great fatigue, exposure and risk, one man **was commonly detailed for the** express duty of carrying whiskey from **the** nearest tavern, not in bottles, but **in** the common "paten' **pail,**" holding ten or twelve quarts, and this man, who was always a sober, steady-going fellow, was charged not to "**ladle**" the liquor **out** too freely. Sometimes, **however, in** the **hurry,** a thirsty chap would contrive to get more than he could rightly carry, and this happened to be the case with the party who volunteered to accompany Duncan on this occasion. Duncan, however, very peremptorily, and to the great chagrin of the man, ordered him to stay on shore and "sober up" as quickly as possible, and selected as his companion an old friend, and well-proved associate in many a scene of peril, of the name of Finlay.

Together they proceeded to give the final tug and heave at the few sticks still jammed in the rapids.

What they dreaded now occurred. The jam suddenly broke before they could leap to the shore, and they were rapidly swept down the river on the struggling, whirling timber. They were safe for the present on a stick which floated somewhat apart from the others, but immediately before them, and a few feet below the bridge, was a succession of such broken and boiling eddies that no man could pass through and live. As they neared the bridge they saw to their relief that a single stick which had floated in advance of them, had got lodged lengthways across from one pier to another, and a chance, though a slim one, was left them for their lives. The point of difficulty was to spring from their own stick on to this one, before they should strike it, for at the speed with which they were being swept along the collision would certainly hurl them headlong into the boiling torrent. Duncan, who was on the end nearest to the transverse stick, made his leap in time, and with success; but not so his companion.

Before he could make the spring the stick struck with the force and velocity of a cannon-ball, and he was violently thrown into the water. Just as he was being swept under the stick on which Duncan was now standing, the latter seized him with his powerful hands by the shoulders, and partially dragged him on to the stick, while his legs and lower part of his body were kept under by the force of the current. And now took place one of the most remarkable " tugs of war" which certainly ever occurred, on that river at least : Duncan pulled and strained with all his might, and though he was one of the most powerful men on the river he could not raise or budge him one inch from the terrible embrace of the current.

By this time the rest of the men had gathered on the bridge, but, though he called loudly for assistance, not a man would venture down to his side. It was indeed a perilous undertaking : the smooth slippery stick was oscillating up and down at a fearful rate in the swollen angry torrent, and a slip and fall would precipitate a man into certain death. At length Dan, Duncan's younger brother, made the hazardous attempt, but even the united strength of the two was utterly insufficient to drag Finlay up and out of the river's death-grasp. And the poor fellow, who was now almost unconscious, begged them to let him go, that they were crushing in his ribs and breast. Duncan, who all this time had retained his coolness and self-possession, and also his determination to save his friend at all hazards, seeing it was impossible to drag him on to the stick, now called to the men on the bridge to throw him the end of a long line, and making a slip-knot of this he managed to pass it over Finlay's feet, and draw it tight round his ankles. Then calling to the men to hold firm, he relinquished his hold on his shoulders, and as the current swept him violently under the stick, the men, with a lusty echoing cheer, hauled Finlay, feet foremost, safely on to the bridge.

But the poor fellow was in a sorry plight, his clothes were all stripped to the skin, and his body, from his heels to his head, was as black as a negro's, and as battered and bruised as if he had passed through a threshing mill. For a week he kept his bed, and was very thankful then to be able to resume his work.

Not infrequently, as we have said, these "chutes" and rapids are the scenes of fearful mutilations and loss of life. Hardly a season passes that the death-roll has not to be called at one or more of these dangerous passages by some "concern." These disasters are often the result of carelessness or wanton recklessness on the part of the victims themselves. They often occur in the following manner: after all the timber has beeen passed through the rapids it is then necessary to transport the provisions, tents, boats, etc., to the foot; this must be done either by carrying and dragging them by the land portage, or running them over the rapids. The men have a great dislike to portaging the heavy canoes or boats; and where it is at all practicable will invariably run them over. But even where it is not practicable but hazardous in the extreme—and by *accident* only they escape with their lives—they sometimes will persist in making the attempt. This is particularly the case if there happen to be any whiskey about; some old drivers, whom a hundred hair-breadth escapes have only hardened and made reckless, will, under its crazing influence, "stump" any one of the gang to run the rapids with him, and often will succeed, by taunts and ridicule, in persuading some other fool to attempt the passage of death.

Some years ago an accident occurred in this way which caused considerable stir at the time, and had, I believe, the effect of checking to some extent these foolhardy exhibitions of insane and reckless bravado. The principal in this affair was a man of the name of Colton, widely known throughout the Ottawa valley for his extraordinary strength, agility, and reckless hardihood. A common feat of his was to take a flying leap on the level, over a team of horses; and in every kind of athletic exercise he was the champion of his day.

The drive to which Colton belonged had all passed over the rapids, the provisions and raft-gear being portaged by the land road, when he was taken with one of his reckless humors, and proposed that they should run the canoes over. The rapids were among the most dangerous on the Ottawa river, just a little above Des Joachims, and ended in a fearful eddy and whirlpool—over them no mortal man had ever yet run and lived. At that time—over thirty years ago—they were in their natural state, but now they have been so improved by side dams and slides that their passage is comparatively easy.

Colton's proposal was at first scouted and laughed at, but such is the cowardice of men in the face of ridicule and taunts, that his persistence finally prevailed on two men to accompany him in the terrible undertaking. Their departure was witnessed with breathless interest by the rest of the gang, which increased to the wildest excitement as the large, heavy canoe bounded like a feather over the foaming, boiling surges of the "chute." Near the foot was a large rock against which the angry waters dashed, and were thrown back in furious seething swells. Notwithstanding the utmost exertions of the men, the canoe was thrown violently against the rock, and was immediately upset by the recoiling waters, and Colton and his companions were precipitated into the whirling torrent, and in a second were hurried into the eddy and whirlpool below. One man managed to grasp the canoe as it shot past him, and was carried safely through into the calm water beyond, but the other two were seized in the deadly embrace of the whirling waters, out of which no human strength was able to escape. Colton's companion, who had probably received some injury when the canoe upset, was immediately drawn under and was seen no more, and his body was never recovered. Colton, however, struggled long and powerfully. Never, perhaps, was there a more fearful struggle for life on the broad, deep waters of the Ottawa. Though the shores were lined with strong stalwart men, accustomed to every peril and accident of river life, yet not an effort could possibly be made for his rescue. All they could do was passively to watch the course of the unequal contest, and fearfully await its certain and terrible issue. Eighteen times was Colton carried round on the whirling circle, and every time he was about to be drawn in by the deathly suction he contrived, by a tremendous exertion of strength, to dive under and out of its reach, only to be again seized by it, when he rose to the surface, and irresistibly drawn towards the gurgling vortex of death. But, finally, his gigantic strength had to succumb, and as he neared the fatal point for the last time he threw up his arms in despair, and, with a fearful cry, that was mockingly re-echoed by the surrounding hills, he sank, and did not again appear.

CHAPTER XXVII.

Sandy C——.

REPRESENTATIVE men of the lumber merchant class have been rapidly changing their character and habits within the last few years.

Formerly it was quite a common thing to find these gentlemen engaging personally, working with their own hands, in the practical business of the concern. They lived in the shanty with the men during the greater part of the winter; they went down the river with them on the drive, and settled up and paid them off with their own hands in Quebec. They knew the name of every Tom, Jack and Bill in their employment, and were "hail-fellow-well-met" with very many of them.

The orthodox doctrine in those days was that no timber business could prosper unless the "boss" was directly at the head of it, and personally superintending every detail of it. Hence he was often the hardest working man in the concern. He was the first in the woods in the morning and the last to return to the shanty at night. If a difficult and dangerous piece of work had to be done he was always on hand with his stentorian "hee-au, hee!" to head the gang who had to perform it. In a jam on the river he always took the post of danger, and was the last man to make his escape to the shore. Physically, as much as in any other sense, he was the head, heart and soul of the whole concern.

We can easily understand how powerful an influence and stimulus in working, such a line of conduct would exert among the men, and how strongly it would tend to keep up the *esprit de corp*, and general good feeling in the shanty, especially if the "boss" were well liked which, we are glad to say, he generally was.

But a mighty change has come over the manners of those gentlemen in these later days of prominence and prosperity in the lumber trade. You no longer find them in their shirt-sleeves with handspike in hand, heading and cheering on the men in every perilous and difficult piece of work. All this, and every other kind of manual and practical work, is now delegated to the foreman. They never think now of staying for weeks and months at a time in the shanty, and bivouacking in the tent by the river side in the spring, as in the good old days.

Their acquaintence with the shanty and the work is limited to an occasional flying visit for a day or two during the winter, when they burst in upon the astonished simple-minded backwoodsers with jingling bells and gorgeous equipages, and all the importance and dignity of a prince of the blood royal. As for the men, they do not pretend to know the names of a quarter of them; and, except with a few old, faithful and privileged fellows, they never exchange a word of greeting or kind fellowship.

I have no intention whatever of drawing any disparaging comparison between these totally different representatives of the same order of men. In new and altered circumstances new modes of procedure and fresh developments of character are presented to view. In the case in point each class of character is suited to its own times and surroundings.

Not only has the lumber trade now assumed such proportions, in its greatly enlarged extent and importance in the country, as to necessitate a much closer attention to its outside and financing departments, both as to supplies and market, than formerly; but the fact is, and in this lies the main cause of this change I speak of, the lumber merchants are connected with and largely carrying on other businesses besides the lumber business proper. The great majority of them have now large saw mills, grist mills, general stores, and, in some instances, extensive machine shops and cloth factories to engage their attention. These interests necessarily so occupy their time and business energies that it is impossible to take the active and personal oversight in the lumbering business which they formerly did. The fact is that with some of them now this business is only a subordinate and auxiliary affair altogether to other and more absorbing ones.

I must confess, however, that my predilections run, as a general thing, in favor of the old class character of lumber merchants. Take them all in all they were noble specimens of humanity—its truest ring found in them its clearest echo. They were manly, upright, open-hearted, and hospitable to a fault. Accustomed to large money transactions they spent freely and lived high, perhaps a trifle too much so. As a rule, they were devoid of that petty trickery and sharp-practice, which in their more genteel brethren of these later days have been engendered by their more intimate association with outside and city life, and more extensive and fluctuating collateral businesses. There is no stronger proof of this than the fact that it was no uncommon thing to find men who had grown gray and often become supernumeraries in the service of the same family; also for men to leave their wages for years in the hands of their masters, feeling it was quite safe there, and they would receive it with interest whenever they choose to ask for a " squaring up."

Prominent among this class of men stands out Mr. Alexander C——, the father of my friend C——. He was generally known under the familiar appellation of Sandy C——, though in his case the oft-times mendacious proverb was proved doubly false, for the more familiarly you knew him the more you respected and admired him. He was no common man in any sense you liked to take him. Though he has been dead for some years, yet he is firmly held in most affectionate and grateful remembrance; and they do honor to themselves who thus remember him. He was a genuine man in the highest sense of the term, and an honor to the class to which he belonged.

He is often spoken of as the pioneer lumberer of these backwoods, though in strict accuracy he was not so, as the Yule brothers were before him and also the Americans who drew timber out of Calabogie Lake as early as 1812, and gave their name to the bay on that lake; but he was the first who reduced the business to a thoroughly systematic, and profitable shape, and laid the foundation of ultimate success and affluent independence for the family. Nearly sixty years ago he commenced life in the woods at the early age of twelve, and for forty years he labored with an indomitable patience and courage, which has certainly never been surpassed in the annals of pioneer hardship and difficulty in Canadian backwoods life. He was pre-eminently a toiler of the forest. Until within a year or two of his death three-fourths of his time was spent in the woods and on the river, sharing the discomforts of the gang in the heaviest and most dangerous work that had to be done. He shirked nothing that any man could do, and did many a thing that the boldest and hardiest wouldn't dream of attempting. He loved the work, and the work loved him; it never soured or aged his temper, but fostered in him all that was kind and genial and manly.

To my mind the perfection of true manhood is the retaining of boyhood and never suffering it to die out while life lasts. A genuine man shews his real manliness just as much in his relaxation from work as in the toughest and stiffest strains of his life. I love to hear the old boyish laugh ring out, and the cheerful peals of a still youthful spirit echoing among the stern crags and buffets of life's realities.

Now such a man was Sandy C———. No one could ever accuse him of negligence in work or duty, nor would he allow it in the smallest degree among his men. In fact, he was generally exceedingly arbitrary and authoritative among them while the work was going on, especially if it was of a difficult and pressing nature. In truth he sometimes went a little too far in this direction. For, while he prided himself on being able to do what any other man could do, he also expected every man under him to do the same. Not infrequently when he saw a fellow remiss, as he thought, he would unceremoniously dislodge him, and seizing axe or handspike do the work himself, and then threaten the man with all sorts of terrible things, if it should ever happen again. He worked his men harder than any " boss " on the river, and yet he was better liked than any other on it, for when the work was done and the press over he was most kind and considerate, and would allow his men every indulgence and join in with them in any frolic or amusement that was going on.

His whole life from his earliest boyhood was so full of stirring incident and adventurous hardship, both in the forest and on the river, that it is difficult

Enterprise and Hardihood (Old School).

to seize upon any specially prominent points to illustrate it. From his earliest days he was a keen sportsman, and always prided himself upon having the best rifle and fowling piece in the backwoods, and was himself a first-class shot with both.

If he happened to be at home in the Fall, during the time that we were having our annual deer hunt, he enjoyed nothing more than spending a few days with "the boys," as he called us, in our backwoods camp; and nothing pleased us more than to have him with us. He was the life of the party, for though he was a merciless despot at getting us up in the morning and off to our posts, still when the hunt and business of the day was over, he was the youngest and keenest among us in any frolic or athletic games that we indulged in.

He had a great dislike to profane language, especially of a blasphemous character. His reverence for the name of the Creator was most profound, and he had no hesitation in checking and rebuking a man when he heard him uttering these profanities. I remember well one time when he and I and another party were about to cross a large lake in a small bark canoe, this person had been indulging rather freely from his flask, and as we were preparing to embark gave utterance to many profane expressions, frequently invoking the name of our Saviour, I saw Sandy's eye gleaming and his wrath kindling till, with a look and a tone that none but he could assume, he burst out, "stop that, sir, such language is not fit for any Christian man to use, and particularly at such a time as this, you ought to be afraid to enter this canoe; stop it!"

The man was at once thoroughly cowed and sobered, and during our passage up the lake sat on the bottom of the canoe without stirring a limb, or uttering a word.

Sandy was as fearless a man as ever breathed; in fact, I believe he did not know what fear was. He lumbered for a number of years on the Trent river, and on one of his visits to a small town on that river he was robbed of a large sum of money. In the course of his business that day he had occasion to visit several of the hotels, and in his usual manner spent freely and lavishly with all whom he met. When he retired to his room at night he found that a package of notes containing about $1,600, which he had carried in his overcoat pocket, was gone. He at once called his clerk who had accompanied him, and on talking over the matter their suspicions immediately fell on the same party. This was a notorious bully and desperado of the town, an ex-convict of the penitentiary, a man of immense stature and strength, and altogether a very ugly customer to deal with. Both Sandy and the clerk had noticed him during the day hanging about them, and particularly if there were any "general drinks" called on, and felt positive he was the culprit. Without hesitation or delay they started for the man's house—Sandy arming himself as he passed through the dining-room with the large carving knife—and rousing him out of bed, Sandy, in a tone of thunder, demanded his money, telling him "he would not leave the house till he gave it up." The ruffian rose and with many an oath denied the charge, and went to seize his gun which was in a corner of the room, but our friend divining his purpose sprang at him, and threatened to put the knife into him unless he at once gave up the money. At this juncture his wife who was lying trembling in the bed spoke up, and told her husband "he might as well own up to the theft, and that the money was actually concealed in the bed tick on which they were lying." At the same moment the clerk made his appearance through the door, and the man seeing himself thus beset on all sides sullenly confessed to the matter, and going to the bed he raised the clothes and brought out a package of bills, and said "a part of it was there and the rest was hidden in the woodshed." While the clerk counted the money, Sandy went with him to the place, determined not to lose sight of him till the whole amount was recovered, and sure enough in a secret recess of the outhouse was the rest of the money; the two sums covered the exact amount he had lost. Sandy told me " he felt so sorry for the poor devil that when he found all was right he handed him a ten dollar bill, telling him to give up his evil courses, and turn over a new leaf." He was greatly offended, however, when I remarked to him that " I had no doubt the scoundrel followed up his advice by giving his wife a tremendous beating as soon as his back was turned."

Take him all in all, Sandy C—— was as noble a type of humanity as ever lived and toiled in the Ottawa Valley, and no memory is held to-day in greater esteem and affection among those who knew him, both rich and poor, than his.

CHAPTER XXVIII.

A Carnival in a Riverside Shebeen.

THIS is to be not a very agreeable chapter to read, and I would advise the delicate minded reader to give it the go-by. But I must write it, else my book would be lacking one of the essential characteristic features of backwoods river life.

Lest my readers should be carried away with too exalted an opinion of the purely heroic in shantyman character and life by what I have depicted, I must, at the expense of what is pleasant and commendable, tell the truth in a somewhat darker shade about them.

Notwithstanding what I have written about the greatly improved 'morality, and general tone of character, and habit of shantymen now, compared with what it used to be, still it can be readily understood by those who know human life and nature that there necessarily must be much that is rough, coarse and even brutal among this class of men.

I deny most emphatically that the general influence of shanty life in the woods during winter is prejudicial in itself to a good, fair tone of character and morals. If anything, apart from perverse extraneous influences, it is the reverse. The plain, strong, healthy food—the pure, keen, bracing atmosphere—the heavy, unremitting physical exertion, the regular routine life week in and week out—and the total abstinence from intoxicating liquors, all combined, have a tendency, if not to elevate, at least not to lower the ordinary standard of human morality.

But I must confess that a certain change takes place in these aspects of character when the drive commences in the spring. The river life is more calculated to unsettle good resolutions and habits, and to develop the harum-scarum propensities of human nature than that of the winter. It is a life of irregular, unsettled and changeful interest, and is beset with new and peculiar temptations to the ex-hibernated shantyman.

If he is grogily inclined, he has now frequent opportunities of gratifying his appetite. Every few miles on the river side there are low taverns, or shebeen shops, licensed and unlicensed, where rank vitriolized poison, under the name of good-whiskey, is sold by the glass or bottle to the thirsty drivers.

These places are hot-beds of abominations. They awaken and revive in full force the long repressed devil of strong drink which has been lying dormant, perhaps almost extinguished, by the lengthy winter sojourn amid the pure bracing influences of the forest. Now it is that, upon occasion at least, the river-man can, if he pleases, give full fling to all that is sensuous, low, and debasing within him. On Saturday nights especially, when the week's work is finished, and he can sleep off the effects of a debauch on the Sunday, these river-side shabeens are often the scenes of frightful orgies, and of most inhuman and brutal "fights" between individuals of the same drive, or free fights between rival gangs of other "drives."

Those encounters in their ferocity, bloodshed, and often serious and even fatal consequences, beggar all description. When the devilish passions of those rough and powerful men are thoroughly roused by the demon of whiskey, then they become more like wild beasts, and infuriated madmen than human beings.

I have never seen the terribly demoralizing effect of strong drink in completely changing the character and disposition of a man more strongly exemplified than among those men, and especially on such occasions. You would not know them to be the same men. You may perhaps have particularly remarked some fellow as being of a most quiet, staid, well-behaved demeanor. He was always up to time in his work, and one of the most peaceably inclined, inoffensive men in the shanty community. He was the last man in the world you would suppose who would strike a blow or give a cross word. But behold him in liquor! and what a metamorphosis? If a veritable saint were to be changed into an incarnate devil you could not be more surprised, and disgusted.

I have in my mind's eye at this moment just such a person, one, alas, among not a few. When I first became acquainted with him, and my continued acquaintance only strengthened the opinion. I thought he was one of the most exemplary and highly to-be-respected men I had ever met with. He carried himself with a grave, self-contained bearing that was impressive in the highest degree. He delivered himself with a sententious gravity, and full toned deliberative utterance that would have done credit to a reverend principal of a Scotch university. He moved about among us with the air and demeanor of a Sir Oracle. There was even an odour of sanctity about him that would have adorned a Congregational minister of the highest standing in the Union. And I really liked and respected the man, and always enjoyed conversation with him. I never heard an oath from his lips; and his opinions, given in his deep-toned, full-measured accent, were always sound and sensible, and what you would naturally expect from his appearance and deportment.

And yet this man, when in liquor, was a perfect fiend. He was quarrelsome, profane, and obscene to the lowest degree. He was looked upon as one of the most noted bullies in the Ottawa Valley, and was the hero of perhaps more "fights" than any man in it. In fact, he never could indulge freely in whiskey without getting into a scrimmage of some kind. He loved a fight for the fight's sake, and if his foul tongue could not provoke a man into a quarrel with him, he would often adopt the most ingenious expedients in order to bring it about. On such occasions he was a man who "had a grievance," and could always rake up some old grudge, either personal or relative, as a plausible pretext for an attack. If he succeeded in his design, woe generally betided his antagonist, for few indeed were able to stand against his tall, powerful, active frame, and his quick ambi-dextrous movements. His fighting was of the genuine wild-cat sort of bruising, nothing fair and stand-up about it, but the meanest, trickiest, most unmanly rough-and-tumbleism. He left no foul means untried to maim and " use up " his opponent. He would kick, bite, trip, and tear like a wild beast, and was just as savage and unsparing in his punishment; marks and injuries would often be left on his victims for life. His favorite mode of attack was, at the first opportunity, to plant a terrible kick with the toe of his heavy boot under the chin of his adversary, and if this fearful blow did not at once disable, it would so stun him as to render him quite helpless, and then he would maul and kick him till he was completely insensible. This " kick " of his, however, was so well known that, except with a perfect stranger, he had seldom the opportunity afforded him of inflicting it.

One of the most sanguinary and hard contested of all his encounters took place at a low tavern, on the mouth of one of the principal tributaries of the Upper Ottawa.

It was in the spring, during the " rafting up " process, that is, the binding together of the single pieces of square timber into " cribs," each containing about twenty-five sticks, which is always done on reaching the Ottawa, for up to this point the timber has been floating in the streams in loose single sticks.

Several concerns had met at this point, and were simultaneously carrying on the business of rafting up; consequently, some hundreds of men were collected at and about the mouth of the river, and a vast amount of drinking, swearing and fighting were continually going on among them at the tavern.

One Saturday night a fearful drunken spree was indulged in by a large number of the "drivers" from the various gangs. It was a beastly carnival of noisy, drunken excess. Highwines diluted with water, and then charged with the oil of vitriol to disguise the water, was the only, and continuous drink. As its maddening fumes rose to the brains of those fearless and powerful men, every species of backwoods coarseness and brutality was exhibited, and even gloried in by the intoxicated river men. Profanity, obscene joking, ribald songs, rough feats of strength, tricks of all sorts, and every now and then a bloody fight, made up the programme of the night's entertainment, and was extended far into the next day. As an eye witness told me, "it was like a little hell on earth."

Prominent as usual among the revelers was the

man we speak of; he was drinking heavily like the rest, and was in "capital twist" for a fight—every other pastime on such occasions being mere child's play for him. All his attempts, however, to pick a quarrel with some one were unavailing, for every one knew what he was after and kept clear of him. At length, though, he got his desire gratified, and one of the most bloody and disgusting hand-to-hand combats followed that was ever known in the Ottawa Valley.

And who do you imagine was his antagonist? **His own brother!**

And what can you possibly conceive was the cause of dispute? Nothing under the sun but simply to prove which was the "best man." This had long been an open question between them, and to-night they mutually agreed to decide it.

The two men were pretty equally matched, though his brother was, if anything, the heavier and more powerful man, but not so quick and active. So in perfectly cool blood and good understanding they went at it, but very quickly they were more like two raging devils, thirsting for each other's blood, than brothers born and nursed by the same mother. For more than three hours the unnatural conflict raged with varying success on each side. Never was the holy stillness of a Sabbath dawn broken by a more inhuman struggle, and one that was within a hair's breadth of stamping the brand of Cain upon one of them. They struck and tore at, and bit each other like infuriated tigers, and locked in one another's iron grasp they frequently rolled over and over on the ground, none daring to interfere, or try to separate them, for this is the rule in such encounters among these men. The beastly, sickening scene was finally terminated by our man getting worsted and having to succumb. And what do you suppose was the cause of his defeat? **His** brother managed to get the thumb of his right hand between his teeth and clenched it there, and held on like a bull-dog until he nearly bit it off, and the other was forced to cry "quits" and give in.

The encounter, however, was very nearly **proving** fatal to him; it was followed by lockjaw, and for six weeks he lay **at** death's door, from which he was only saved by the almost superhuman strength of his constitution.

Whatever may be the extenuating circumstances in a man for gratifying his fighting propensities while inflamed and brutalized by whiskey, I know of none whatsoever, nor have I the slightest sympathy or consideration for the recognized "professional" shanty **bully—the man who,** in liquor or sober, in the shanty **or on** the drive, is always ready **for a** fight and trying to provoke one. It is a character of which the possessor, no matter what victories he may gain, has no reason to be proud, but, if he had **any** sensible discernment, to be thoroughly ashamed of. He is **admired and** feared only by the mean, the ignorant and the cowardly, while all sensible, right-thinking people utterly despise him and, if they choose to take **the** trouble, can very quickly **dispose of,** and put him down, for at the best he **is** only a sheep in **wolf's** clothing, and a coward **at heart. He is the pest** of shanty life, and **a** detriment **to its peace, comfort** and right **working,** and the sooner **he is disposed** of **in any** practicable way the **better** for all parties concerned.

The "bully" is a man that has no real friends, **but** many most substantial enemies; and before **long he finds** out that **his** career has been a mistake, **and has** gained for him nothing but disappointment, **contempt and misfortune.**

CHAPTER XXIX.

Shooting the Rapids and Slides of the Grand River.

IT is quite a common thing when you are speaking to these backwoods river-men about the Ottawa, for them to ask "is it the Grand River you mean?" for by this and no other name will they recognize and designate it. The origin of this name is traceable, as far as I can ascertain, to the earliest days of Canadian history. When Jacques Cartier, the gallant, noble and Christian navigator of imperishable memory, caught his first glimpse of this magnificent river, in a burst of joyous pride he exclaimed " *La Grande Rivière.*"

Ottawa, however, is the old Indian, and of course proper, name; and if pronounced according to the Indian dialect the accent should be placed upon the second syllable, and would thus sound Ot-tà-wa. The Ottawa is one of the grandest rivers on the American continent, and in common with most of the rivers of this country is diversified with high falls, boisterous rapids, and beautiful cascades. Over these or alongside of them, in long "slides," the timber has to pass on its way from the forest to the market at Quebec.

As I have before said, the timber is floated in single pieces down all the numerous tributaries of the Ottawa, and then is " rafted-up " at " the mouth " of each. The rafting-up process is an arduous and stirring piece of work, generally occupying several days, and requiring great skill and experience on the part of the foremen. The timber " sticks " are bound together, according to size and length, into cribs, each one containing twenty-five pieces, and these cribs are again bound together, though in a manner easily to be unloosed, into " drams," or " bands," sometimes called, each dram containing about twenty-five cribs; these drams again bound together make up a " raft," which is then in a shape for towing in sufficiently deep and broad waters. The timber is made up into cribs for the sake of shooting the slides, and into drams for the running of the rapids.

Shooting the slides on cribs is capital sport; in its excitement and velocity it reminds you of tabogganing. Two men manage the crib, one at the stern, the other at the bow, who, with their immense oars, steer it fair for the mouth of the slide, and, catching the current, it glides down the steep incline with immense rapidity; so great indeed is its velocity that it often completely submerges itself in the calm water below. When you shoot **the** slides you should have your top boots on, if you wish to keep your feet and legs dry.

Shooting the **Chaudière** slides at Ottawa is a favorite **amusement with** adventurous visitors, but it is **not** unattended with danger, especially to nervous ladies. I would advise no one to undertake it **except in company** with some lumbering friend, and on a carefully-selected crib, and one strongly bound together. If you can manage to get on the "cookery **crib,**" which carries all the provisions and cooking utensils, then **you** may consider yourself quite safe, as **it is** constructed with all the skill and care that the most experienced raftsmen can bestow.

But for exciting amusement and soul-stirring **adventure, commend me to** running the rapids on the drams. This is the grandest sport on the river for the tourist, and the hardest work for the "drivers." The rowing that has **then** to be done by these men is the toughest strain upon their muscles of any of their whole year's work. The oars, which are thirty feet long, and about a hundred pounds in weight, are placed at the stern and bow, and the whole force of the crew—and at some rapids of special danger many extra hands are engaged—is divided between these two places. As the dram in its headlong descent approaches some dangerous spot, as a rock or reef, or shoal, the pilot, who stands about the centre, gives a shout, or a motion of his hand when his voice can't be heard, and then each man must bend to his oar, and tug and strain as if his life hung on it. And, in fact, it practically may, for if, through any weakness in the rowing or any mistake of the pilot, the dram should deviate from its proper course and strike upon a shallow reef or projecting point, then almost certain destruction would overtake the whole concern. The furious rushing torrent would soon break it up into single pieces, the bindings of withe, rope, and chain would snap like thread, and the immense sticks would be whirled about, and down the rapids like straws.

If this should happen, then every man must look out for himself; and though loss of life sometimes occurs, yet, such is the agility and wonderful skill of these men in sticking to the smooth, slippery timber, that they generally escape to the shore, or to the foot, through the boiling rapids.

But, barring these accidents, running the rapids is the most stirring of all river sports; it is exhilarating in the highest degree, and gives, what is never to be despised in life, a new sensation. As the heavy, unwieldy mass dashes into and through the high foaming swells, which often break over the bow, and submerge half the dram, the loud cries and violent gestures of the pilot, the wild hurrahing of the men, the creaking and twisting of the timbers beneath you, and the tumultuous swish of the boiling waters, all combined with the race-horse speed at which you plunge ahead, make up a scene of excitement and delightful exhilaration that can never be forgotten, and ever after awakens a thrill of pleasant remembrances.

There is one rapid in particular over which I have had many a delightful run, and which is associated in my mind with many pleasant reminiscences. It is the Long Sault, between Grenville and Carillon. It was until very lately the terror of the raftsmen, both on account of its length (nearly twelve miles) and several points of special danger. But these are now greatly diminished by the Government dam, built across the river at Carillon, and the erection of slanting piers at the dangerous spots, so that running the rapids now is only child's play compared with what it formerly was.

I remember once when running these rapids a most ludicrous, though it might have been a most fatal, incident occurred, which for the time "set the raft in a roar." The hero of the affair was an awkward, clumsily-built fellow, who was always busy with things he had no business with, and continually in the very place where he ought not to be. He was a regular Handy Andy sort of chap, and never out of scrapes of some kind or other. On this occasion he would persist in taking his stand on the outside stick of timber—a place that is seldom occupied in these dangerous rapids. As the raft approached the Trois Roches, one of the most dangerous spots, and the pilot, as is usual in such cases, ordered the men to pull in their oars and run back to avoid the bursting swells, this man persisted in keeping his position, and pulling away as lustily as ever. And, as was to be expected, just as he was bending for another stroke, a mighty swell struck the long broad blade of his oar and dealt him such a lusty blow with the handle that he was suddenly thrown several feet into the air, and, turning a complete somersault, he came violently down on the broad of his back on the hard timber. While every one was looking on in breathless consternation, expecting that in another instant he would be swept from the raft by the rushing swell, he suddenly regained his feet, and, as if he had been made of India-rubber instead of flesh and bones, bounded from the spot and darted into his cabin, and as he aftewards said, never knew where he was until he found himself deeply ensconced under the blankets and heard outside the uproarious bursts of laughter and merriment. It was as narrow an escape, however, as a man could possibly have in such circumstances. If he had been stunned by his heavy fall on the hard timber, as any ordinary reasonable mortal should have been, he would in another second have been swept over the edge of the raft into the rapids, where no human aid could have assisted him. But fools and drunken men seem to be under the guardian care of some special providence, whether of Heaven or Satan I cannot say.

When the timber by crib and dram has passed through the rapids and slides and broad waters of the Ottawa, and been fairly launched into the majestic bosom of the St. Lawrence at Lower Laprairie, behind Montreal, then it is made up for the last time into one large compact raft and towed without impediment or hindrance, except, perhaps, a storm on Lake St. Peter, into the booms at Quebec ; and the toils, adventures, and hardships of the raftsmen are over for another year.

CHAPTER XXX.

Settling up in Quebec.

THE "settling up" in Quebec is an anxious time for both the lumber merchant and the shantyman.

The former has now to square his accounts for the year, to take stock of his expenditures, and the quantity and quality of his timber after the wear and tear of the drive, and the probabilities of the market, to find out how he stands in the world.

For the past year it has been a continual outlay of money without the return of a single cent. A hundred or more men have had to be fed during that time, perhaps as many horses during the winter; timber licenses, Government dues, slidage, interest on capital paid for limits, and a hundred other expenses peculiarly incidental to the lumbering business, have been draining his pockets for the last twelve months. The year's expenditure from the time the first tree has been cut in the fall, until the whole raft has been passed over into the hands of the buyer at Quebec, foots up a heavy sum, all gone in hard cash.

There is no business that I know of in which there are so many and such large demands upon the purse as that of the lumber merchant. No wonder, then, he is anxious about the state of the market, which perhaps is the most uncertain and fluctuating of any in the world. A European war, a depression in stocks, a rise or fall in Turkish or Egyptian bonds, a score or more of causes, may so operate as to make or mar a fortune for the lumberman. And such is the nature of the business that these gentlemen are not satisfied, like ordinary mortals, with a fair and reasonable profit; no, they expect a bonanza with every recurring season. A few thousands will not do; they look for tens and scores of thousands to stand at the foot of the balance sheet to their credit when the year's business is wound up. And very often, if they cannot get the price they want, they will let their timber lie over for another year, and, if their means can hold out, for yet another, if the market is not to their liking. I have known cases in which the merchants have held on for five years, in the hope that the market would rise to the standard of their lofty expectations. When, finally, they do sell it is often either an avalanche of ruin, or a reflux of enormous profit. The lumbering business is something like Indian life, either a feast or a famine, or, like gold mining, a million or nothing.

But what about the men with whom we have more specially to deal in this work? This, also, is a time of anxiety for them, but only up to the moment of being paid off. As soon as the raft is "snubbed" within the booms at Quebec, and put in its most presentable shape for the inspection of the buyers, then the "boss" comes aboard with a bag of money, and with his clerk pays to each man the amount coming to him. Very many of these fellows, especially the French, can neither read nor write, and are in a state of uncertainty as to the actual amount coming to them; their account for clothes, tobacco, advances to their families, dockings for lost time, etc., have in most cases made a considerable hole in their year's wages, in some instances entirely eaten it up, with even a balance against them. But in general there is a pretty fair sum coming to them, varying in amount from a hundred to three and even four hundred dollars. Sometimes there may be a hot row between the parties, when some man thinks he has been wrongfully charged with advances or lost time; but almost invariably the boss has the better of the dispute, for while the poor fellow has nothing but his memory, or counting upon his fingers, to rely upon, the mysterious entries in the clerk's book tell dead against him, and the boss summarily closes the matters by telling him "to take it or leave it, just as he likes," and calling up another man. As a general thing, however, there is very little difficulty in settling, and the moment Bill, Pat, or Louis receives his money his anxiety is over, and, like a boy out of school, he is ready for any fun or frolic that may turn up.

Like **Jack Tar when** he gets into port, the poor shantyman has **now to** run the gauntlet of the very **worst** and vilest temptations that can assail a man. For the **past ten months** or more he has toiled, take it all in all, as no other class of working men have to do; during that time he has led, as a rule, a careful, abstemious, saving life, twenty-five dollars would probably cover all his necessary personal expenses. Under the wholesome influences of rigid discipline, arduous but healthy work, abstinence from intoxicating stimulants, and continual life in the open, bracing air, one would naturally suppose that both mind and body would be so tempered and strengthened as not only to be able to withstand the strongest temptations to vicious and sensual indulgence which the flesh and the devil could present, but also to have a positive distaste and repugnance to them. And so it would be with well-balanced, high-toned and rightly-trained dispositions; but, alas, few of the shantymen possess these offsets against temptations to aid them in maintaining these wholesome influences of the past year's life. In the revulsion of their position from restraint and abstemiousness, there is also a revulsion of their feelings as to indulgence and licentiousness. In the first burst of his absolute freedom and idleness the thoughtless shantyman is too apt to go headlong into every indulgence that presents itself, and you may be very sure the devil is at his elbow to help him on. As he leaps with a light heart and a heavy pocket from the raft on to the shore he is at once beset with a host of hell-runners in the shape of calash drivers, boarding-house agents, brothel sirens, and crimps and sharpers of the blackest stamp. "Come and have a drink, my jolly buck," is generally the first salutation that greets his ears, and in the joyous hilarity of his soul, the poor fellow thinks it only "good manners," and right fellowship to comply; and though with many an inward resolution to take care of himself, and many a knowing wink to himself that he knows what he is about, he soon becomes helplessly entangled in the devilish wiles of those who, with-

out pity or remorse, will strip him of his last shilling.
He supposes that he may take a few glasses with
perfect safety, and have a good time for a day or
two, and then draw off and go to his home or work,
none the worse in body or pocket. But Satan never
palmed off a blacker deception upon human credulity
than this which the shantyman imposes upon himself. The liquor with which he is plentifully plied
is poison of the blackest and rankest kind, and on
account of his long abstinence from all intoxicants
produces a more immediate and potent effect than
it otherwise would. As the fiery spirit mounts to
his brain, and his pulses, already exhilarated, become
doubly so under its influence, he soon loses all
caution and self-command. His love of ostentatious
spending and open-handed treating give themselves
full fling—he treats right and left, and delights in
being the hero of a thirsty crowd of spongers and
thieving vagabonds, and flourishes his bank notes
and tosses them on the counter with the air and
tone of a millionaire. Of course the upshot of the
whole business can be readily surmised. Between
bad whiskey and worse men and women he is
plucked as clean as a Christmas goose, and in an
incredibly short time too. I have known several
instances of men who have received between two

and three hundred dollars, coming back to their employer before twenty-four hours without a cent in their pocket, and in the direst distress and shame begging to be taken out of this "cursed hole," and have their passage paid back to their homes or to Ottawa. There are numberless cases of the most deplorable weakness and folly in this connection that have ever been recorded, and not infrequently with men of most decent and well-behaved character,—very often men who had not the remotest intention or desire to go on "a spree," as they call it; but in the circumstances we have mentioned, which it would take almost a saint to withstand, have been led and egged on by those wily fiends until a whole year's savings are gone, and they are stripped and beggared, in some cases actually plundered and almost beaten to death.

These open-hearted, free-handed men, flush with money and the self-confidence of redundant health and spirits, are like children in the hands of these cunning pitiless crimps that dog their steps from the moment they set foot in Quebec until their last cent is gone, when they are remorselessly kicked into the street and sent about their business.

Now in this connection there is one of the most clamant fields for the exercise of philanthropy and charity which at the present time exists in our country. We have our homes and institutes for sailors at almost every port; there are reading rooms, coffee houses and soup kitchens for all classes of working and indigent men and women of the community, but nothing has ever been done in the way of care and kindness for the shantymen—a class of our countrymen who, for peculiarity of character and habits, susceptibility of kind and good influence, as well as for numbers and business importance, have the very highest claims upon our consideration and sympathy. There is a scheme which has been in my mind for years, and concerning which I have conversed with many lumber merchants, and great numbers of the men in almost every section of the Ottawa Valley, and which, with all deference, I would submit to the kindly and, I hope, favorable consideration of the benevolent and charitably-minded both of Quebec and Ottawa.

It is this : " the establishing a kind of savings bank in Quebec into which the wages due to the men would be paid by the employers on the arrival of the raft at that city. The deposit of these moneys to be made on the following conditions, viz.: that they shall be sent to the men on their arrival at their homes, or to their families, if they wish, or held in security for them in any way that may be deemed best at a fair rate of interest, until such time as they should ask for it, but always on the understanding that it cannot be drawn out in Quebec, either in person or by proxy." The great point and benefit of such an institution will be at once patent to the most superficial reflector. It provides a safe-guard for this most interesting and peculiar class of our countrymen at the **hour of** their most peculiar and powerful temptations. **It tides over for the** time, and **this the** most perilous of their year's work, the terrible dangers, both to pocket and morals, to which they are exposed at the hands of the basest, most degraded and unscrupulous class of our community. There is not in all the land a more clamant call upon the benevolent sympathies and practical assistance and counsel of **our kindly-disposed Christian men** and women than this, and that, **with a** little judi**cious** management, could be more easily responded to.

In the carrying out of such a scheme a great deal of nicety of detail and of business tact and knowledge would be requisite, but, if it could be done, the incalculable benefit to the shantymen **will at** once be seen.

Suppose a committee of the leading clergymen of

the city, both Catholic and Protestant, would be formed and meet together; they could soon devise the practical steps for the carrying out of the plan. The greatest difficulty would be in securing the consent and co-operation of the men to such an institution. Two objections will at once be taken by them. 1st. Their natural independence and boldness of character will at once prompt them to say : "we are quite able to take care of ourselves and of our money too in Quebec, and, besides, we want some relaxation and indulgence when the work is over for the year." 2nd. Their fear that, through some mismanagement of the institution, they might not get their money when they needed it, or possibly might lose it altogether.

As to the first objection, I have no hesitation in saying that in time it would be entirely got over. I have talked over the matter with great numbers of these men both in the woods and on the river, and I have almost invariably found that it meets with their full concurrence, and would be regarded as a great kindness and benefit to them as a class. A very common opinion expressed by them was this, "only give it a start; say only twenty men went into it the first year, and they found it worked well, the next year a great many more would follow their example, and before long, when the scheme was thoroughly understood and its benefits realized, it would become very generally adopted. But let the 'boss' give the men some money when they get to Quebec, say a fourth or a sixth of what is coming to them, enough to have some reasonable diversion and to carry them to their homes, and lodge the balance to their credit in the bank. There is hardly a man but what in time would go into the scheme most heartily on these terms, and be more and more thankful at the end of every year that he had done so."

As to the 2nd objection, viz., security to the men for the money deposited, that would be a matter of business detail and cautious judgment with the committee.

No doubt an arrangement could be made with the Post Office Savings Bank, or any safe institution, for the deposit, profitable using, and safe transmission of the money to the proper parties at the specified time. We venture to affirm that if three or four influential business gentlemen of Quebec, who had a desire to do a good and kind turn to their countrymen of this class, would undertake this matter, and co-operate with the lumber-merchants, who, I know, would give their hearty approval to the scheme if it was fully and fairly set before them, they would soon put it in a practical, safe and manageable position. The time and trouble involved on their part would be very small indeed compared with the incalculable benefit, both moral and pecuniary, to the shantymen. In all probability after two or three years' trial the enterprise would stand, and be worked on its own merits. The shantymen, realizing the safety and benefit of the scheme, would do their own business at the bank, and voluntarily engage not to draw the money until they or their families really needed it. If only a fair proportion of those men would be induced to deposit their earnings in this way the gross amount would be a most profitable addition to the working capital of any bank, even though it should be for only a few weeks, and enable it to pay a fair interest to the depositor.

But we must remember that a large number of these men have no family or other claims upon them for their wages; outside of their own personal requirements they do not need to expend a single cent of their whole year's earnings. Consequently many of them would, in all probability, leave their money in the bank until their return on the following year, and then add to it another year's income. And such is the action of human nature in affairs like this, that when they actually realized that they had saved their year's wages, or the best part of it, they would be stimulated to save more the next year. There is no case in which the old adage "money makes money" is better proved than just in such a connection with this class of people. When they found that a sum of money, say two hundred dollars or more, which otherwise would have been squandered on strumpets and grog shops, was lying snug in the bank at a good rate of interest they would at once perceive the wisdom of the course they had pursued, and it would thus be the best practical incentive to them to behave themselves, and save their money another year.

We would strongly advocate the extending of this benevolent institution, though with somewhat different modifications, to the City of Ottawa.

Ottawa is the great "hiring depot" of the lumbering region. To this city the merchants or their agents come to engage men for the next season's work.

Work in the woods generally commences about the middle of September—up to this time, therefore, after being discharged at Quebec a month or six weeks previously, and having their "spree" over, if they will have one, the men are either at their homes in the country or, if they have none, boarding in Ottawa until they are hired again.

This period is, of course, a harvest time for boarding-houses and low grog shops in Lower Town, and, consequently, with too many of the shantymen, a time of rioting, and spending what money may be left after their Quebec escapades. Even though a man may not have a cent of money when he comes to Ottawa, those boarding-house sharks will receive him with open arms, and give him all he asks for, knowing right well that when re-engaged all his bills will be paid by the merchant, who, of course, in turn deducts the amount out of the man's pay as the season goes on. Many a man while idling away his time at these places spends beforehand his whole winter's wages. In fact, in numberless cases, the Quebec experience, both on the part of the shantyman and his despoilers, is here re-enacted.

Here, then, is a grand field for the exercise of benevolent and philanthropic activities. If nothing else, a shantyman's boarding-house should be established, on the same principle as the sailor's institutes in London and Liverpool, where these men can be comfortably and cheaply lodged, and generally looked after during the few weeks they require to stay in Ottawa. Such an institution would be of incalculable benefit in every way, and, equally with the Savings Bank in Quebec, would, after its benefits have been proved and realized, be hailed by the shantymen as an inestimable boon. The experiment has been a wonderful success in London with sailors, and, from what I know of the characters and feelings of shantymen, would prove equally, if not far more so, with them.

Reader, my book is finished. If I have told you anything new about Shanty, Forest and River Life that has interested or, perhaps, instructed you; if I have awakened any warmer feeling in your heart for the sublime scenery and unutterable pathos of our lonely Canadian backwoods; above all, if I have called forth a single kindly thought, and any truer appreciation of the simple-hearted, open-handed, manly toilers of the forest, then I will consider my study and labor in this work amply repaid, and that I have not toiled in vain.

END.

Merchant Tailor,

206 St. James Street,

MONTREAL,

Keeps on hand a Stock of Goods suitable

For Sporting Suits, Hunting, Boating or Yachting,

Also every class of Goods

FOR GENTLEMEN'S WEAR,

MADE ON SHORT NOTICE.

———

Samples supplied to Intending Purchasers.

T. COSTEN & CO.,

302 Notre Dame Street,

GUN and FISHING TACKLE MAKERS,

IMPORTERS OF

W. W. Greener's Hammerless and Trap Guns,

ALSO

Winchester, Colts' & Kennedy's Magazine Rifles,

Colts' & Wesson's Double Action Revolvers,
38, 44 and 45 Cal.

Ballard's, Wesson's and other Single Rifle,
Suitable for Deer and Moose Shooting, always in Stock.

Fishing Tackle,
In Great Variety.

Forrest & Son's Salmon and Trout Rods, Salmon and Trout Flies,
Of the most Improved Patterns, such as :

Jock Scott, Silver Doctor, Fary and Rangers.

Split Bamboo, 8 oz. Fly Rods.

D. Scribner & Sons' Salmon and Trout Rods,
Made of the Best Greenheart.

New Castle Chilled Shot.

Curtes & Harvey's Grain Gunpowder.

Joseph Rogers & Son's Celebrated
Pocket Cutlery and Hunting Knives.

W. DRYSDALE & CO.'S

CATALOGUE

OF

STANDARD AND MISCELLANEOUS

BOOKS,

COMPRISING A LARGE SELECTION OF THE BEST AND LATEST

BRITISH PUBLICATIONS,

WILL BE SENT TO ANY ONE, ON APPLICATION.

Montreal:

W. DRYSDALE & CO., BOOKSELLERS AND STATIONERS,

232 St. James Street.

TEACHERS' & SCHOLARS' HELPS.

WEEKLY.

Sunday School Times..$2.00 per annum.
Scholar's Weekly Lesson Paper ....$7.20 per 100   "

MONTHLY.

Notes on S.S. Lessons..............45c. single copy, or $30.00 per 100 per annum.
S.S. Banner........................65c.   "   "   60.00   "   "
S.S. World.........................60c.   "   "   50.00   "   "
Westminster Teacher...............60c.   "   "   50.00   "   "
Scholar's Lesson Paper.................................... 6.00   "   "
Primary Paper... 6.00   "   "
Westminster Lesson Leaf .... 6.00   "   "
 "   Primary " .... 6.90   "   "
Berean Leaf... 5.50   "   "

QUARTERLY.

S.S. Union Quarterly....................................$20.00 per 100 per annum.
Scholar's   "   .... 25.00   "   "
Peloubet's   "   .... 20.00   "   "
Westminster   "   .... 15.00   "   "
Quarterly Review Service................................... 9.00   "   "
Canadian Scholar's Quarterly............................... 8.00   "   "
Berean Leaf Cluster................................$5.25 single copy per annum.

Half Hours with the Lessons, 1884, $1.50.
Vincent's Notes, 1884, $1.25.
Peloubet's Notes, 1884, $1.25.
Monday Club Sermons, 1884, $1.50.
Westminster Bible Dictionary, $1.50.
Schaff's Bible Dictionary, $2.50.
Cassel's Bible Dictionary, $2.50.
Westminster Question Book, 1884, 15c. ; by mail, 17c.
Rice's Scholar's Hand-Book, 1884, 18c. ; by mail, free.
Vincent's Class Books, 1884, Senior, Intermediate, Beginners, 18c. each ; post free.
Sunday School Schemes, 1884, 60c. per 100.
Book Mark Lesson Lists, 1884, 50c.   "

MONTHLY ILLUSTRATED PAPERS.

Name of Publication.	Price per single copy.	Price per 100 in City.	Price per 100 by Mail.
Adviser................................	25c.	$12.50	$15.00
Apples of Gold	50c.	40.00	40.00
Band of Hope........................	25c.	12.50	15.00
Boys' and Girls' Companion...........	45c.	25.00	30.00
British Evangelist..................	45c.	30.00	30.00
" Workman.................	45c.	25.00	30.00
" Workwoman...............	45c.	25.00	30.00
Canadian Band of Hope................	25c.	15.00	15.00
Child's Companion....................	45c.	25.00	30.00
" Paper.....................	30c.	12.00	12.00
" Bible Companion..........	45c.	30.00	30.00
" Own Magazine.............	25c.	12.50	15.00
Children's Friend....................	45c.	25.00	30.00
" Paper.....................	25c.	12.50	15.00
" Messenger.................	25c.	12.50	15.00
" Record....................	25c.	12.50	15.00
China's Millions.....................	45c.	30.00	30.00
Christian Friend.....................	45c.	30.00	30.00
Cottager.............................	45c.	25.00	30.00
Crystal Stories......................	45c.	25.00	30.00
Dawn of Day..........................	25c.	12.50	15.00
Early Days...........................	45c.	25.00	30.00
Family Friend........................	45c.	25.00	30.00
Faithful Words.......................	45c.	25.00	30.00
Forward..............................	40c.	25.00	25.00
Friendly Visitor.....................	45c.	25.00	30.00
Herald of Mercy......................	25c.	12.50	15.00
Infant's Magazine....................	45c.	25.00	30.00
Juvenile Missionary Magazine.........	25c.	12.50	15.00
Morning Star.........................	30c.	6.00	6.00
Missionary Juvenile..................	45c.	25.00	30.00
My Little Friend.....................	25c.	12.50	15.00
My Sunday Friend.....................	25c.	12.50	15.00
My Paper.............................	30c.	11.50	11.50
Prize................................	45c.	25.00	30.00
S.S. Presbyterian....................	25c.	13.00	13.00
S.S. Visitor.........................	25c.	12.00	12.00
Sunbeam..............................	50c.	25.00	25.00
Things New and Old...................	45c.	25.00	30.00
Voice to the Faithful................	45c.	30.00	30.00

www.ingramcontent.com/pod-product-compliance
Lightning Source LLC
Chambersburg PA
CBHW032044220426
43664CB00008B/858